Sport in the Americas

Statues of fans as nostalgic monuments to the North American devotion to baseball, Canadian lacrosse and ethnic ideologies, the rise of modern sports and class sensibilities in São Paulo, the inaugural world championship for women's hockey, and national memories of Olympic Games hosted on US soil. What do these seemingly disparate themes have in common? They each comprise a facet of sporting experiences in the western hemisphere that took place between the 1890s and the 1990s.

This collection offers new insights on the role of sport in defining local, regional, national, and international cultures in the western hemisphere. The essays offer historical perspectives on the power of sport to create common ground in modern societies while simultaneously exploring how it serves to mark cultural boundaries and reinforce cultural identities. From national pastimes to ethnic traditions, from class sensibilities to racial ideologies, *Sport in the Americas* presents novel contributions that examine both the singular and manifold patterns of culture that sport animates.

The chapters in this book were originally published as a special issue in *The International Journal of the History of Sport*.

Mark Dyreson is a Professor of Kinesiology and History at the Pennsylvania State University, USA; the Director of Research and Educational Programs at the Penn State Center for the Study of Sports in Society; the Managing Editor of *The International Journal of the History of Sport*; a former President of the North American Society for Sport History; and a Fellow of the National Academy of Kinesiology.

T0347518

Sport in the Global Society: Historical Perspectives

Series Editors: Mark Dyreson, Thierry Terret and Rob Hess

Historicizing the Pan-American Games
Edited by Bruce Kidd and Cesar R. Torres

Olympic Perspectives
Edited by Stephan Wassong, Richard Baka and Janice Forsyth

Media, Culture, and the Meanings of Hockey
Constructing a Canadian Hockey World, 1896–1907
Stacy L. Lorenz

Methodology in Sports History
Edited by Wray Vamplew and Dave Day

Olympics in Conflict
From the Games of the New Emerging Forces to the Rio Olympics
Edited by Zhouxiang Lu and Fan Hong

The Sports Development of Hong Kong and Macau
New Challenges after the Handovers
Edited by Brian Bridges and Marcus P. Chu

Martial Arts in Asia
History, Culture and Politics
Edited by Fan Hong and Gwang Ok

Sport in Europe
Edited by Annette R. Hofmann

Sport in the Americas
Local, Regional, National, and International Perspectives
Edited by Mark Dyreson

For more information about this series, please visit:
https://www.routledge.com/Sport-in-the-Global-Society---Historical-perspectives/book-series/SGSH

Sport in the Americas

Local, Regional, National, and
International Perspectives

Edited by
Mark Dyreson

LONDON AND NEW YORK

First published 2018 by Routledge

2 Park Square, Milton Park, Abingdon, Oxfordshire OX14 4RN
52 Vanderbilt Avenue, New York, NY 10017

Routledge is an imprint of the Taylor & Francis Group, an informa business

First issued in paperback 2020

British Library Cataloguing-in-Publication Data
A catalogue record for this book is available from the British Library

ISBN13: 978-1-138-48148-0 (hbk)
ISBN13: 978-0-367-53155-3 (pbk)

Typeset in Minion Pro
by codeMantra

Publisher's Note
The publisher accepts responsibility for any inconsistencies that may have arisen during the conversion of this book from journal articles to book chapters, namely the possible inclusion of journal terminology.

Disclaimer
Every effort has been made to contact copyright holders for their permission to reprint material in this book. The publishers would be grateful to hear from any copyright holder who is not here acknowledged and will undertake to rectify any errors or omissions in future editions of this book.

Contents

Citation Information

The chapters in this book were originally published in *The International Journal of the History of Sport*, volume 32, issue 14 (August 2015). When citing this material, please use the original page numbering for each article, as follows:

Chapter 1
Standing Out from the Crowd: Imaging Baseball Fans through Sculpture
Christopher Stride, Ffion Thomas and Gregory Ramshaw
The International Journal of the History of Sport, volume 32, issue 14 (August 2015)
pp. 1611–1641

Chapter 2
Reclaiming Canada Through Its 'Ancient' Sport: Lacrosse and the Native Sons of Canada in Late 1920s Alberta
Robert Kossuth and David McMurray
The International Journal of the History of Sport, volume 32, issue 14 (August 2015)
pp. 1642–1660

Chapter 3
The Rise of Modern Sport in Fin de Siècle *São Paulo: Reading Elite and Bourgeois Sensibilities, the Popular Press, and the Creation of Cultural Capital*
Edivaldo Góis Jr, Soraya Lódola and Mark Dyreson
The International Journal of the History of Sport, volume 32, issue 14 (August 2015)
pp. 1661–1677

Chapter 4
'Women Can't Skate that Fast and Shoot that Hard!' The First Women's World Ice Hockey Championship, 1990
Patrick A. Reid and Daniel S. Mason
The International Journal of the History of Sport, volume 32, issue 14 (August 2015)
pp. 1678–1696

Chapter 5

Region and Race: The Legacies of the St Louis Olympics
Mark Dyreson
The International Journal of the History of Sport, volume 32, issue 14 (August 2015)
pp. 1697–1714

For any permission-related enquiries please visit:
http://www.tandfonline.com/page/help/permissions

Notes on Contributors

Mark Dyreson is a Professor of Kinesiology and History at the Pennsylvania State University, USA; the Director of Research and Educational Programs at the Penn State Center for the Study of Sports in Society; the Managing Editor of *The International Journal of the History of Sport*; a former President of the North American Society for Sport History; and a Fellow of the National Academy of Kinesiology.

Edivaldo Góis Jr earned a PhD in Physical Education at Gama Filho University, Brazil, in 2003 and is a Professor in the Physical Education Post-Graduate Programme at Unicamp, the University of Campinas, Campinas, Brazil.

Robert Kossuth is an Assistant Professor in the Department of Kinesiology and Physical Education, University of Lethbridge, Canada. His primary research area is the history of sport, recreation, and leisure practices in late nineteenth- and early twentieth-century Canada, with a focus on local and regional histories and how physical culture provides an avenue to explore questions related to masculinity (gender), social class, and race in nascent prairie communities.

Soraya Lódola earned an MA at São Paulo Methodist University, Brazil, and is a Researcher in the Institute of Geosciences and in the History of Science Research Group Unicamp at the University of Campinas, Campinas, Brazil.

Daniel S. Mason is a Professor with the Faculty of Physical Education and Recreation and Adjunct with the School of Business at the University of Alberta, Alberta, Canada.

David McMurray is Professor in the Department of History, University of Lethbridge, Lethbridge, Canada.

Gregory Ramshaw is an Associate Professor in the Department of Parks, Recreation and Tourism Management at Clemson University, USA. He explores the social construction and cultural production of heritage, with a particular interest in sport-based heritage. His research has been published in numerous academic texts and journals, including the *International Journal of Heritage Studies*, the *Journal of Heritage Tourism*, *Current Issues in Tourism*, and the *Journal of Sport & Tourism*, amongst many others. He is the editor of *Sport Heritage* (2015) and is the co-editor of *Heritage, Sport and Tourism: Sporting Pasts – Tourist Futures* (2007) and *Heritage and the Olympics: People, Place and Performance* (2014), all published by Routledge. He also serves on the editorial boards of *Event Management*, the *Journal of Heritage Tourism*, and the *Journal of Sport & Tourism*.

Patrick A. Reid currently works at the Faculty of Physical Education and Recreation, University of Alberta, Canada. He does research in Qualitative Social Research, Molecular Biology, and Genetics. Patrick is the former Vice President of the CAHA and was the Event General Manager for the 1990 WWHC.

Christopher Stride is a Senior Lecturer and Statistician at the Institute of Work Psychology, University of Sheffield, UK. He has published across a wide range of social science disciplines, even poking a toe into pure science or humanities upon occasion, and is particularly interested in the use of statistical methods to support and add rigour to research in areas where advanced quantitative analysis would typically be considered an anathema.

Ffion Thomas earned a PhD at the University of Central Lancashire, UK, with research interests in football and baseball. Her scholarship considers the motivations, significance, and impact of football clubs moving stadia, and in particular the visual culture associated with such moves. She is a Co-Instigator of the University of Sheffield's Sporting Statues Project, which since 2011 has studied the proliferation of statues of sportspeople in the UK and worldwide.

Series Editors' Foreword

Sport in the Global Society: Historical Perspectives explores the role of sport in cultures both around the world and across the timeframes of human history. In the world we currently inhabit, sport spans the globe. It captivates vast audiences. It defines, alters, and reinforces identities for individuals, communities, nations, and the world. Sport organises memories and perceptions, arouses passions and tensions, and reveals harmonies and cleavages. It builds and blurs social boundaries—animating discourses about class, gender, race, and ethnicity. Sport opens new vistas on the history of human cultures, intersecting with politics and economics, ideologies and theologies. It reveals aesthetic tastes and energises consumer markets.

Our challenge is to explain how sport has developed into a global phenomenon. The series continues the tradition established by the original incarnation of *Sport in the Global Society* (and in 2010 divided into *Historical Perspectives* and *Contemporary Perspectives*) by promoting the academic study of one of the most significant and dynamic forces in shaping the historical landscapes of human cultures.

In the twenty-first century, a critical mass of scholars recognises the importance of sport in their analyses of human experiences. *Sport in the Global Society: Historical Perspectives*, provides an international outlet for the leading investigators on these subjects. Building on previous work and excavating new terrain, our series remains a consistent and coherent response to the attention the academic community demands for the serious study of sport.

Mark Dyreson
Thierry Terret
Rob Hess

Sport in the Americas: Local, Regional, National, and International Perspectives

Mark Dyreson

Statues of fans as nostalgic monuments to the North American devotion to baseball, Canadian lacrosse and ethnic ideologies, the rise of modern sports and class sensibilities in São Paulo, the inaugural world championship for women's hockey, and national memories of Olympic Games hosted on US soil. What do these seemingly disparate themes have in common? They each comprise a facet of sporting experiences in the western hemisphere that took place between the 1890s and the 1990s.

That century witnessed the broad diffusion of modern forms of sport throughout the immensity of the Americas, from Tierra del Fuego to Alaska. An import from Europe, particularly from Great Britain, modern sports had taken root in much of the western hemisphere by the 1890s. Clubs, modelled on British originals and devoted to all manner of activities from association football to crew, from athletics to horse racing, from cycling to swimming, sprouted not only in English colonies and former colonies but also in realms that had once been a part of Spanish, Portuguese, French, and Dutch empires in the so-called 'New World'.[1] On one level, modern sports integrated the many nations of the Americas into a unitary culture. A track meet in São Paulo looked very much like a track meet in Santo Domingo or St Louis or Saskatoon. In 1896, when a cabal of European elites led by France's Baron Pierre de Coubertin launched the inaugural modern Olympics in Athens, the western hemisphere was a key component of this cosmopolitan new cultural endeavour.[2] Two 'Americans', José Benjamín Zubiaur of Argentina and William Milligan Sloane of the United States, served on the original International Olympic Committee that started in 1894 and staged the renewed spectacle.[3] The United States sent a large contingent, while Chile sent a single athlete. Canada, Cuba, Haiti, and Mexico sent athletes to the 1900 Olympics in Paris, while Brazil and Colombia also made claims that their citizens competed—an issue that was not as cut and dry in this early stage of the Olympic movement as it would become as the games became larger and better organized. By the 1920s, North, South, and Central American nations regularly sent teams to the Olympics.[4]

The western hemisphere played a key role in the rise of a global sporting culture, not only in the Olympics but also in the pastime that became the 'world's game'—association football. Uruguay won Olympic championships in association football in 1924 and 1928, and then hosted the first global tournament, the World Cup, in 1930—defending its title with a victory of Argentina. By the 1990s, several other western hemisphere nations had hosted the globe at the World Cup, including Brazil, Chile, Mexico, and the United States.[5] By the 1950s, the Pan American Games, contested every four years, provided the western hemisphere with its own multisport gala.[6] During the century between the 1890s and the 1990s, the western hemisphere also hosted six summer Olympics and four winter Olympics.[7]

Sport connected the Americas to a larger global culture. Sport also served to bind the nations of the western hemisphere together in a common set of pastimes and competitions.

Modern sport thus served as common structure for providing shared experiences among a disparate collection of nations with different historical traditions, social organizations, and languages tied otherwise mainly by geography. While sport provided unitary cultural experiences for the Americas, it also provided platforms for the expression of a myriad of national, regional, and local cultural traditions. Indeed, the very term football, or *fútbol* in Spanish or *futebol* in Portuguese, described very different games in different places and different times.[8] The United States altered British football codes and relegated association football and rugby football to niche markets while developing their own unique version of 'American' football. Canadians took the 'American' version of the game and tweaked it into a Canadian alternative.[9] Association football became an impassioned devotion of the masses in Latin America. Each Latin American nation developed its own particular flavour of the game: the technical proficiency of the Argentines, the creative élan of the Brazilians, the synthetic blend of control and flamboyance of the Mexicans.[10] Other national and regional sporting cultures have proliferated. Cricket flourished in the British regions of the West Indies, while the US-invented game of baseball thrived in the Spanish-speaking areas of the Caribbean.[11] Cycling became a national pastime in the vertiginous landscapes of Colombia, while sprinting has blossomed in Jamaica.[12] Many American nations have sports centred on cattle-ranching heritages, each with its own national flourish, from rodeo in the United States to *charreada* in Mexico to *coleo* in Venezuela and Colombia.[13] Canada invented two national pastimes, hockey and lacrosse, both of which have crossed the border and become significant sports in the United States.[14]

Modern sport has not only served to link the Americas into a global and transnational culture but has also provided spaces for the growth of vibrant national, regional, and local cultures. Such is the mysterious plasticity of sport in the modern world. It serves both to unite and to divide, to promote transnational connections and to nurture tribal bonds. The essays in this collection illuminate the dualistic nature of modern sport as simultaneously singular and manifold.

In 'Standing Out from the Crowd: Imaging Baseball Fans through Sculpture', Christopher Stride, Ffion Thomas, and Gregory Ramshaw examine the cultural memorialization in bronze of the 'common folk' who flock to stadiums in the United States and Canada. The authors catalogue the artistic, historical, and commercial imperatives that create these commemorations of fandom and place the statues firmly in the historic tradition of baseball's enduring efforts to market itself as an essential national pastime that transcends ethnic, racial, class, and generational boundaries. In 'Reclaiming Canada Through Its "Ancient" Sport: Lacrosse and the Native Sons of Canada in Late 1920s Alberta', Robert Kossuth and David McMurray chronicle another episode from the history of national pastimes. They explore the ironic embrace of a game that claimed connections to the aboriginal inhabitants of Canada, the 'First Nations', by the Native Sons of Canada, white nationalists who preached an anti-immigrant 'Canada First' ideology in the province of Alberta. In this particular case, the Native Sons used lacrosse in an attempt to build a culture that privileged and protected native-born Canadians over recent arrivals from Central and Eastern Europe in the struggle for jobs and resources. Their efforts to promote lacrosse as a 'national' game for native-born Canadians of Western and Northern European ancestry ultimately failed. However, their attempt illuminates the power of sport to forge parochial as well as inclusive cultural identities.

In 'Reading Elite and Bourgeois Sensibilities, the Popular Press, and the Creation of Cultural Capital', Edivaldo Góis, Jr., Soraya Lódola, and Mark Dyreson chronicle the emergence of modern sporting culture in *fin de siècle* São Paulo. As the Argentine city became a major economic centre on the Atlantic Rim, the elites and middle classes, both native and immigrant, found in the newly globalized taste for British-style sporting clubs a set of social organizations that promoted their political and economic interests. Wealthy Paulistas (as the inhabitants of São Paulo dubbed themselves) used sporting clubs to build political and economic networks to maintain their leadership of the region. The cultural sensibilities inculcated through the clubs marked members as cultivated and progressive citizens of the modern West. In turn-of-the-century São Paulo, sport invigorated local, regional, national, and international cultural sensibilities.

In '"Women Can't Skate that Fast and Shoot that Hard!" The First Women's World Ice Hockey Championship, 1990', Patrick A. Reid and Daniel S. Mason chronicle the late twentieth-century re-emergence of women's hockey in North America, focussing on the inaugural Women's World Hockey Championship staged in Ottawa. Reid and Mason document the gender conflicts that marketing women's hockey for public consumption created. They analyze the difficulties of carving out a space for the women's game in the masculinized world of hockey and credit the Ottawa world championships with legitimizing the sport, not only among Canadian audiences but also for powerful international sports organizations, including the International Ice Hockey Federation and International Olympic Committee. Their essay surveys hockey's role in regional, national, and international cultures.

Finally, in 'Region and Race: The Legacies of the St Louis Olympics', Mark Dyreson revisits the much ridiculed and almost forgotten 1904 Olympics in St Louis. He argues that the St Louis games had a more important influence on the future of the Olympic movement, especially in the United States, than most historians have understood. St Louis began the tradition of regional cities that inhabited the periphery of US civilization using the Olympics to market themselves as nationally important centres and global destinations. In the United States, an Olympic hosting pattern developed in which 'new' metropolises, such as St Louis, Los Angeles, and Atlanta, sought and staged the Olympics rather than older, well-established cities, such as New York, Philadelphia, or Boston. These regional dynamics also influenced the ways in which racial conflicts complicated the Olympic experience in the United States. Region and race shaped the production of Olympic spectacles in the United States, complicating the focus on national and international culture that the Olympics inevitably create with regional and local issues.

This anthology of essays on sport in the Americas, grounded in the 'cultural turn' that has concentrated contemporary studies of sport on the interpretive power of culture in human experience, provides new insights into the history of modern societies.[15] The essays analyze the mysterious plasticity of modern sport and offer novel insights into simultaneously singular and manifold patterns of culture that sport animates. The collection seeks to explore sport as both local and global, universal and insular.

Notes

1. Allen Guttmann, *Games and Empires: Modern Sports and Cultural Imperialism* (New York: Columbia University Press, 1994); Allen Guttmann, *Sports: The First Five Millennia* (Amherst, Massachusetts: University of Massachusetts Press, 2004); Joseph L. Arbena and David G. LaFrance, eds., *Sport in Latin America and the Caribbean* (Wilmington, DE: Scholarly Resources, 2002); Joseph L. Arbena, *Sport and Society in Latin America: Diffusion, Dependency, and the Rise of Mass Culture* (New York: Greenwood Press, 1988); David Sheinin, *Sports Culture in Latin American History* (Pittsburgh, PA: University of Pittsburgh Press, 2015).
2. David Young, *The Modern Olympics: A Struggle for Revival* (Baltimore: Johns Hopkins University Press, 1996); John J. MacAloon, *This Great Symbol: Pierre de Coubertin and the Origins of the Modern Olympic Games*, 25th anniversary ed. (London: Routledge, 2008).

3. César R. Torres, 'Mass Sport through Education or Elite Olympic Sport? Jose Benjamin Zubiaur's Dilemma and Argentina's Olympic Sports Legacy', *Olympika: The International Journal of Olympic Studies*, 7 (1998): 61–88; John A. Lucas, 'Professor William Milligan Sloane: Father of the United States Olympic Committee', in *Umbruch und Kontinuität im Sport: Reflexionen im Umfeld de Sportgeschicte: Festschrift für Horst Ueberhorst [Transition and Continuity in Sport: Reflections on the Environment of Sports History: Festschrift for Horst Ueberhorst]* (Bochum: Universität Brockmeyer, 1991).

4. Mark Dyreson, *Making the American Team: Sport, Culture and the Olympic Experience* (Urbana: University of Illinois Press, 1998); César R. Torres, 'Tribulations and Achievements: The Early History of Olympism in Argentina', *International Journal of the History of Sport*, 18, no. 3 (September 2001): 59–92; César R. Torres, 'The Latin American 'Olympic Explosion' of the 1920s: Causes and Consequences', *International Journal of the History of Sport*, 23, no. 7 (November 2006): 1088–1111.

5. David Goldblatt, *The Ball is Round: A Global History of Football* (New York: Viking, 2006); Bill Murray, *The World's Game: A History of Soccer* (Urbana: University of Illinois Press, 1996).

6. Bruce Kidd and César R. Torres, *Historicizing the Pan-American Games* (London: Routledge, 2017).

7. Mark Dyreson, 'The Playing Fields of Progress: American Athletic Nationalism and the St. Louis Olympics of 1904', *Gateway Heritage*, 14, no. 2 (fall 1993): 4–23; George R. Matthews, *America's First Olympics: The St. Louis Games of 1904* (Columbia: University of Missouri Press, 2005); Mark Dyreson, 'The Endless Olympic Bid: Los Angeles and the Advertisement of the American West', *Journal of the West*, 47, no. 4 (fall 2008): 26–39; Mark Dyreson and Matthew Llewellyn, 'Los Angeles Is the Olympic City: Legacies of 1932 and 1984', *International Journal of the History of Sport*, 25, no. 14 (December 2008): 1991–2018; Tim Ashwell, 'Squaw Valley: 1960', in John E. Findling and Kimberly D. Pelle, eds., *Historical Dictionary of the Modern Olympic Movement* (Greenwood, CT: Greenwood Press, 1996), 263–269; Kevin B. Wamsley and Michael K. Heine, 'Tradition, Modernity, and the Construction of Civic Identity: The Calgary Olympics', *Olympika: The International Journal of Olympic Studies*, 5 (1996): 81–90; Kevin B. Witherspoon, *Before the Eyes of the World: Mexico and the 1968 Olympics* (DeKalb: Northern Illinois University Press, 2008); Terrence Teixeira, 'The XXI Olympiad: Canada's Claim or Montreal's Gain?: Political and Social Tensions Surrounding the 1976 Montreal Olympics', in Stephen Wagg and Helen Lenskyj, eds., *The Palgrave Handbook of Olympic Studies* (London: Palgrave/Macmillan, 2012), 120–133.

8. Bill Murray, *The World's Game: A History of Soccer* (Urbana: University of Illinois Press, 1996); Janet Lever, *Soccer Madness* (Chicago: University of Chicago Press, 1983); Tony Mason, *Passion of the People? Football in South America* (New York: Verso, 1995); Roger Alan Kittleson, *The Country of Football: Soccer and the Making of Modern Brazil* (Berkeley: University of California Press, 2014); David Goldblatt, *Futebol Nation: A Footballing History of Brazil* (London: Penguin Books, 2014).

9. Tony Collins, *Oval World: A Global History of Rugby* (London: Bloomsbury, 2015); Andrei Markovits, and Steven L. Hellerman, *Offside: Soccer and American Exceptionalism* (Princeton, NJ: Princeton University Press, 2001); Mark Dyreson and Jaime L. Schultz, *American National Pastimes—A History* (London: Routledge, 2015); Frank Cosentino, 'A History of Canadian Football, 1909–1968' (M.A. thesis, University of Alberta, 1969).

10. Mason, *Passion of the People?*

11. Hilary Beckles, *The Development of West Indies Cricket* (Barbados: Press University of the West Indies, 1998); Michael M. Oleksak and Mary Adams Oleksak, *Béisbol: Latin Americans and the Grand Old Game* (Indianapolis, IN: Masters Press, 1996).

12. Héctor D Fernández l'Hoeste, Robert McKee Irwin, Juan Poblete, *Sports and Nationalism in Latin/o America* (New York: Palgrave Macmillan, 2015); Richard Moore, *The Bolt Supremacy: Inside Jamaica's Sprint Factory* (New York: Pegasus Books, 2017).

13. Richard W. Slatta, *Cowboys of the Americas* (New Haven, CT: Yale University Press, 1994).

14. Donald M. Fisher, *Lacrosse: A History of the Game* (Baltimore: Johns Hopkins University Press, 2002); Ken Dryden and Roy MacGregor, *Home Game: Hockey and Life in Canada* (Toronto: McClelland and Stewart, 1989); Richard Gruneau and David Whitson, *Hockey Night in Canada: Sport, Identities, and Cultural Politics* (Toronto: Garamond Press, 1993); Andrew Holman, *Canada's Game: Hockey and Identity* (Montreal: McGill-Queens University Press, 2009).

15. Jamie L. Schultz, 'Sense and Sensibility: Pragmatic Postmodernism for Sport History', in R. Pringle and Murray Phillips, eds., *Critical Sport Histories: Paradigms, Power and the Postmodern Turn* (Morgantown, WV: Fitness Information Technology, 2013), 59–76.

Standing Out from the Crowd: Imaging Baseball Fans through Sculpture

Christopher Stride, Ffion Thomas and Gregory Ramshaw

Sculptures of athletes that immortalize heroic feats have long been part of the sporting world. More recently, statues of sports fans have appeared, particularly at baseball stadiums across North America. Whilst athlete statues usually represent specific subjects, fan statues typically depict anonymous figures, giving commissioners and sculptors broader license to incorporate particular ideals. This paper investigates how the fan statuary's form reflects commissioners' motivations, values, and views of fandom, and whether fan statues promote a preferred (but often imaginary) narrative regarding the fan experience. A tripartite fan statue design typology is proposed: hero worship, family experiences, and the crowd. By examining an example of each type, with context provided by a unique database of baseball statuary, the fan statuary's predominant themes and tensions are illustrated. Fan statues are concentrated at Minor League ballparks, and all feature children. The majority are alloys of both real and imagined components of the idealized fan experience of the baseball organization's 'ideal fan', projecting inclusive, family-friendly, and timeless game day experiences, and evoking nostalgia for childhood. Crowd-type statues offer a more free-spirited and spontaneous aesthetic, with the crowd creating and becoming part of the spectacle – a reality that sports organizations may be less comfortable with.

Sculptures of athletes that immortalize heroic feats have long been part of the sporting world, with figurines dating from 1400 BC depicting contestants of the Mesoamerican ballgame and Greek classical statues of athletes at Olympia from the sixth and fifth centuries BC (most notably Myron's 'Discobolus') amongst the most prominent ancient examples.[1] In the present day, they are ubiquitous across a wide range of sports, including soccer, basketball, and American football, and have a global reach.[2] Baseball statues are particularly abundant, forming the most prolific national single-sport statuary, which currently numbers over 230 monuments across the USA; there are also small numbers (< 10 per country) in other baseball nations such as Puerto Rico, Korea, Japan, and Mexico.[3] However, the subjects of baseball's monumental tributes are also no longer confined to heroic players and their professional supporting cast of managers, executives, and broadcasters. Unlike fans of almost all other sports, and in numbers far greater than fans of any other sport, baseball fans are now being depicted in sculptural tributes (the only other sport to have embraced fan statues is soccer, with a handful of examples in the UK, Russia, Mexico, and most notably Spain).[4] As of 1 July 2014, 21 statues featuring baseball fans had been unveiled, most of which are located at Major and Minor League ballparks.[5]

The recent development of sports statuary, notably at major stadia but also in urban centres, museums, and commercial premises, is attracting an increasing level of academic enquiry.[6] Historians Mike Huggins and Mike O'Mahony comment, in their treatise on the role of the visual in sport history, that 'Increasingly ... there has been a greater recognition of the centrality of the visual for a deep understanding of sport'.[7] This development reflects how the material artefacts of sport, such as statues, offer a lens upon the sports organizations', fans', and players' cultures, and indeed wider societal histories, fashions, and mores. In their selective readings and recreations of the past and their heterogeneous interactions with the present, monuments usually tell us more about the cultures, values, and hierarchies of those who erect them and view them than about the subject of the statue itself.[8]

Whilst any sports statue may potentially hold these properties, the baseball fan statuary offers a particularly fertile area of exploration. Across the 21 fan statues or statue groups that currently exist, all but 2 of the 57 individual sculpted fan figures are fictitious or anonymous.[9] Therefore, compared to the wider statuary of players, managers, and executives, which is overwhelmingly subject-specific (and must therefore have some degree of verisimilitude through portraying known people with recognizable features, playing styles, and histories), the relative anonymity provided by fan statues gives statue promoters, funders, and sculptors far greater scope for interpretation, manipulation, and presentation of an image or idea. It follows that using iconography and iconology to consider the design, detail, and presentation of baseball *fan* statuary rather than the player statuary offers a potentially sharper, less compromised insight into the commissioning sport organization's ideals and ethos.

Statues of storied sports figures have been variously cited as the products of nostalgia-based marketing strategies that bask in the glory and accomplishments of past players, provide a totem of authenticity in a modernized and rationalized stadium environment, and create a distinct organizational, local, or national identity – or as a public statement of reparations.[10] They may also reflect a desire for a more public alternative to the cemetery or graveyard as a place for mourning deceased heroes.[11] Yet, these motivations are unlikely to be primary drivers behind the construction of fan statuary. A fan, even if depicted lauding his or her team's victory, cannot reflect a sports organization's glory as effectively as a player cast in heroic action, or a manager lifting a trophy. A fan's anonymity, even when contextually clothed in period uniforms and equipment, renders him or her as a less effective (if not entirely empty) repository of reminiscence, and a less meaningful landmark than a real figure's image, or moment that potential viewers will have experienced personally or via folkloric tradition. Neither is erecting a fan statue instead of aggrandizing a player likely to be an economically driven compromise. Whilst statues of players are typically single subject, every fan statue we have identified contains two or more figures, thus inflating the cost of sculpture and casting. Therefore, distinct and fresh motives are likely to exist for imaging fans, and for doing so in a public sculptural format.

Furthermore, the combination of sculpture with fans as the primary subject is a recent phenomenon without historical precedent. Indeed, it is debateable whether there has previously been any consistent genre-specific depiction of baseball fans. Baseball-related artworks date back to the dawn of the game itself and, as Allen Guttmann notes in his treatise on American sports art, include 'thousands of painted, carved, and cast images', mostly by marginal or unknown artists.[12] However, at least amongst artworks by major figures or with wider public recognition, such as Thomas Eakins' painting 'Baseball Players Practicing' from 1875, or 'Three Base Hit' by James Henry Daugherty, the player, the game, or the whole ballpark scene has been the focus, with the fan or crowd in the grandstands providing the backdrop.[13] Fans have likewise been included in murals at contemporary ballparks and as part of local art projects, but are again usually limited to a background role.[14]

As such, this new form of artistic representation of fans poses a number of questions and avenues that are ripe for inquiry. First, what motivations exist for organizations to erect fan statues? The cost of a mural is likely to be dwarfed by that of a multi-figure bronze statue. Second, what do the form and detail of fan statues tell us about their commissioners and patrons, particularly the commonalities and differences in Major and Minor League baseball organizations' views of actual and ideal fandom? Third, do these portrayals bear comparison with reality, or are these statues being used to promote an alternative, preferred but imaginary narrative regarding the fan experience?

Our examination of fan statues reveals a threefold design-based typology, each element of which describes a different aspect or experience of the fan body: hero worship by child fans, the family experience, and the fan as a collective being, i.e. the crowd. A detailed investigation of an exemplar of each type, coupled with reference to characteristics of wider fan statuary, illustrates the overarching themes and tensions present across these design types. 'Child/player' and 'family' statues are primarily marketing tools created by sports organizations, concentrated at Minor League facilities, and erected to attract fans both through promoting an accessible, inclusive, and family-friendly game day experience and by evoking nostalgia for childhood. Such monuments are alloys of real and imagined components of idealized fan experiences, as experienced by a sports organization's 'ideal fan'. Conversely, the less common crowd-type statues, which are typically civic funded, project a more rebellious, free-spirited, and spontaneous aesthetic, one in which the crowd has power to create and form part of the spectacle – a reality with which sports organizations are often less comfortable.

The Fan in Baseball

Psychologist Daniel Wann defines a sport fan as 'an individual who is interested in and follows a sport, athlete or team'.[15] Regardless of whether he or she attends games, it is an interest and commitment in following the sport or team that sets them apart from those who witness a sporting event but do not identify with what they are watching – 'spectators' or 'consumers'.[16] As baseball historian Fred Stein posits in his history of baseball fandom, a spectator differs from a fan in requiring 'little or no effort to shake any emotional reaction to the result of a game in which he has little more than a passing interest'.[17]

The motives behind an individual's decision to establish and maintain his or her participatory status as a 'sport fan' have been extensively researched.[18] Wann categorizes these motives into multiple distinct types.[19] Two revolve around the social aspects of attending a sports event, namely the potential to share time and space with family, and to experience group affiliation through the opportunity to spend time with likeminded others. The enjoyment of the skills and aesthetics of the event witnessed is a third motivation. Fourth, fans often view their favourite team as an extension of themselves, experiencing the 'thrill of victory' when their team wins and the 'agony of defeat' when their team loses. Both the arousal experienced whilst watching a game, and the boost to self-esteem through watching their team perform well and triumph, incentivize their fandom – though, as Matthew Klugman notes, the more committed fans will also experience deep disappointment at their team's failure to achieve goals that have become, by association, their own 'objects of desire'.[20] Being a fan may also offer escape (a diversion from everyday life), entertainment (sport as an enjoyable pastime), or even economic advantages through gambling on the event.

Sport fans engage with their favourite sport or team at different levels of intensity. Marketing researchers Daniel Funk and Jeffrey James describe a psychological continuum model for fandom, consisting of stages of awareness, attraction, and attachment, which may progress to a final state of allegiance.[21] In this latter state, the connection to a sports team 'becomes resistant, persistent, biased cognition – and influences behaviour'.[22] For the professional sports organization, essentially reliant on fans for its income through multifarious channels, encouraging prospective and current fans to move towards allegiance, the state in which they will attend and consume the most is of fundamental commercial importance. In other words, with the ever-present churn in a fan base making its constant replenishment essential to the organization's financial survival, every sports organization will want to encourage and stimulate fans to identify with their team as strongly as possible. The extent of team identification may be the most important psychological factor impacting attendance.[23] Highly identified, loyal fans are more likely to attend their team's games than are less identified fans.[24] Whilst these fan characteristics and corresponding organizational aims can be generalized to any professional sports organization, it is also true that, like all sports, baseball can be thought of as having a distinctive fan culture influenced by its geographical, sociological, and historical origins, style, arena of play and the stories passed down through the generations. The origins of baseball spectatorship are synchronous with the development of organized baseball in the New York area during the mid-nineteenth century. In a few decades, the numbers of participating cities and fans of the new sport increased at a rapid pace. The advent of admission charges, occurring as they did in conjunction with improved facilities and many players taking on professional status, did not hinder the game's popularity – and although the turn of the century saw an extended period of mismanagement-driven stagnation, the formation of the American League in 1903 established Major League Baseball (MLB) as 'a truly integral part of American life'.[25] Over 100 years later, after experiencing a drawn-out restructuring and expansion to 30 teams, with previously unimaginable developments in technology, player salaries, and stadia, and despite the many alternative entertainment options available, America's 'national pastime' remains a mass spectator sport. In 2013, total MLB attendance topped 74 million, with every member franchise boasting a ballpark capacity above 35,000.[26]

Within the Major Leagues, the uniquely prolonged nature of a 162-game regular season, supplemented by post-season play-off games, both reinforces this status, yet also makes the baseball fan who never misses a game a rare entity. The likelihood is that a large percentage of the fans at any one game will be making a sporadic visit to the ballpark, as opposed to, for instance, an American football game where the balance of supply and demand created by a 16-game regular season means that almost every seat at the most popular teams will be occupied by a season ticket holder. At a baseball game, the crowd at any one game is more likely to be made up from a wide-ranging base of potential attendees. Stein states, 'devoted baseball fans have always included people from all walks of life, income levels, and social strata'.[27] Those attending MLB games tend to have knowledge and interest in the team-related experiences of the event, and are therefore invested in the result.[28] Due to its length and structure, baseball offers perhaps the most leisurely game day experience of the US 'big-four' sports (the others being football, basketball, and ice hockey), allowing for moments of conversation, analysis, and discussion in ways that other major US sports do not.[29] Nonetheless, the focus on the on-field action in MLB makes each major play – such as a home run, great catch, or disputed umpire decision – a collective and often intense experience for those watching. Diversions, such as promotions and stadium concessions, are important but ultimately secondary to the on-field product.

It would be a mistake to assume that an MLB game reflects the baseball fan experience and profile at every level of the sport.[30] MLB forms the summit of a pyramid of Minor Leagues (MiLB) and independent leagues, the former encompassing the affiliated development or 'farm' teams of the 30 Major League franchises, the latter operating outside MLB auspices. Widely spread across the towns and cities of the USA, MiLB and independent league baseball offer fans located away from a Major League city the chance to potentially witness the stars of the future. However, the MiLB or 'indie' game day is very different from its big-time counterpart. The surroundings are more intimate and accessible (MiLB ballpark capacities within the USA range from a few thousand to just under 20,000), and the season consists of fewer games. Whilst every MLB game can be followed live by the omnipresent radio, television, and online coverage, and franchises earn more through shared and individual broadcasting and merchandise contracts than game tickets (i.e. indirectly from fans who are not actually attending the games), MiLB or independent league games are rarely televised, and organizations rely on game day attendances for the bulk of their income.[31] MiLB players are transitory – they are aiming to be 'promoted' to MLB level, unlike the team they represent. Within farm teams, playing strategies will prioritize player development ahead of winning, with the player payroll fulfilled by the associated Major League franchise.

It is the extent to which the majority of fans focus on the result, the relative transience of players and fans, and the contrasting importance of game day ticket sales that underlie differences in how MLB and MiLB baseball franchises will conceptualize fans and seek to attract them. MiLB has a greater economic need for game day fans yet, with their playing roster assigned by their Major League affiliate, and with outstanding performers likely to be moved on to a higher class of baseball at short notice, MiLB franchises can rarely market their games primarily through the competitive spectacle or star batters or pitchers, as might be the case in MLB.[32] In fact, appealing primarily to hard-core baseball fans in the Minor Leagues is, according to one MiLB owner, a sure-fire way of going out of business.[33] MiLB franchises aim to attract as many people as possible to the ballpark itself, primarily by attracting family groups through scheduling (MiLB schedules are not dictated by TV contracts), pricing, and promotions. MiLB provides an inexpensive afternoon or evening out where the fan might watch a ballgame, but that game forms a backdrop to the ice cream, post-game fireworks, and meeting the mascot on the concourse.[34] As Jim Melvin, former ownership partner of the Class A Greensboro Grasshoppers, states, 'Minor League baseball is not about baseball. It's about inexpensive family entertainment'.[35] Because of this, although MiLB teams will have a hard-core of committed fans, many game-goers, attracted by the social experience and game day promotions as opposed to (or without even knowing much about) game-related factors, such as the players or league standings, may best be classified as spectators rather than fans – or alternatively, as fans of the game day experience as much as of the team.[36] Sportswriter John Feinstein aptly illustrates the frequent indifference that some MiLB spectators have to the on-field action, providing several examples of the near-anonymity of former MLB players toiling in the Minor Leagues (a scenario which understandably can breed resentment amongst fallen stars).[37]

Fundamentally, game day fans form a more constant thread in, and are more essential to a MiLB franchise's survival than the players, who are transient and largely divorced from the economics of the franchise. Conversely in MLB, it is the fans that are more transient over the course of a season. The star players who attract game day fans, and more critically, television viewers, radio listeners, and merchandise consumers through their personal performance and contribution to team successes, are the economic levers of an MLB franchise.

Yet, baseball organizations at both the higher and lower echelons of the game are united in that they benefit from the fan behaving as a passive consumer.[38] Just as the importance of the fan to a baseball organization is likely to be reflected in whether they are considered worthy of depiction at all, the organization's perception of its 'ideal fan' will influence which parts of the fan demographic and which aspects of fan behaviour are depicted. In particular, the fans as a collective, i.e. the crowd, present both an alternative, potentially problematic conceptualization of fandom. Though the crowd offers a sense of belonging that fans will appreciate, and vocal encouragement for the pitchers and hitters, this support is not unconditional; fans may turn against a team or player that is not performing. Ultimately, whilst a positive crowd atmosphere offers benefits, a baseball organization's control over fan behaviour and choreography of the game day experience is reduced by the crowd's size and potential to spontaneously create an alternative game day narrative that may not fit with the organization's aims and image. Baseball historian Donald Dewey, writing on fan culture, suggests, 'Like the mass entertainment industry it specialises in, baseball history has found it convenient to idealize or caricature the fan (the father soft-tossing in the backyard with his son) as some entity removed from the fans (the T-shirted fools spilling beer over one another as they reach over the railing to grab a ball still in play)'.[39] Franchise marketing, if not quite aiming to divide and rule, is incentivized to focus on the fan as a singular entity or family group. The crowd as an entity, whether to be exploited or sidestepped, is primarily a Major League phenomenon, given the Minor League baseball's lower attendances and weaker fan engagement with players, game situation, and result.

Fan Statues: Incidence and Typology

An inventory of North American-located baseball statues that feature images of fans is given in Table 1, detailing location, unveiling date, commissioner, funder, sculptor, and design features. Though 58% of subject-specific player statues are sited at MLB ballparks, compared to 13% at Minor League stadia, just under a quarter of fan statues can be found at current MLB facilities, with over half located at MiLB or independent league venues.[40] Fan statues can be classified into three subtypes based upon the experience depicted: child fans with players (or executives), family groups, and crowd scenes.

Child-player designs, which we consider as the first element of a typology of fan statues, combine the fan statue genre with traditional baseball statue subject selection. Figurative sculptures of specific baseball players are ubiquitous across the ballparks of North America. Geographical coverage is not allied to a breadth of visual interpretation, with designs largely restricted to two principal templates: as of 1 July 2014, almost three-quarters portray playing action, with a further 15% of statues depicting a posed player or teammates. However, such orthodoxies are challenged by the aforementioned infrequent but steadily accumulating variant, in which a player is joined on the plinth by sculptures of anonymous child fans. The anonymity of the fans portrayed may posit their presence as equivalent of 'extras' in a bronze biopic, yet the decision to cast them alongside a player, the exalted nature of the players who have received this tribute, and the consistent imagery, marks their inclusion as a further dimension of the artwork as beyond mere decoration.[41]

Table 1 In situ North American statues featuring baseball fans as of 1 July 2014, listed in chronological order of unveiling

Statue	Location	Location type[b]	Sculptor	Date	Promoter	Funder	No. of fans	Gender of fans	Ethnicity of fans	Age of fans	Is specific subject depicted?	Type of statue
1. Jackie Robinson and fans[a]	Parc Olympique, Montreal, PQ	MLB ballpark[c]	Jules Lasalle	16 May 1987	Civic	Civic/Baseball club	2	Male	Mixed	Children	Yes (player)	Children-player/Executive
2. The Audience	Toronto Blue Jays, Rogers Centre, Toronto, ON	MLB ballpark	Michael Snow	3 June 1989	Civic	Civic	15	Mixed	White	Mixed	No	Crowd
3. Jackie Robinson and fans[a]	Jackie Robinson Ballpark, Daytona, FL	Minor League ballpark	Jules Lasalle	15 September 1990	Civic/Commercial	Individual/Commercial	2	Male	Mixed	Children	Yes (player)	Children-player/Executive
4. Take Me Out to the Ball Game	Cleveland Indians, Progressive Field, Cleveland, OH	MLB ballpark	Ron Dewey	4 April 1994	Baseball club	Baseball club	2	Male	White	Mixed (family)	No	Family
5. Hometown Hero	Lansing Lugnuts, Cooley Stadium, Lansing, MI	Minor League ballpark	Richard Hallier	5 April 1996	Baseball club/Individuals	Baseball club/Individuals	3	Mixed	Mixed	Mixed	No (though includes anonymous player)	Children-player/Executive
6. Baseball, a Family Tradition	Arizona Diamondbacks, Chase Field, Phoenix, AZ	MLB ballpark	Clarke Riedy	31 March 1998	Baseball club	Baseball club	3	Mixed	White	Mixed (family)	No (though includes anonymous player)	Family/Children-player/Executive
7. Samuel Plumeri and fans	Trenton Thunder, Waterfront Park, Trenton, NJ	Minor League ballpark	James Gafgen	15 April 1999	Baseball club	Baseball club	2	Male	White	Children	Yes (executive)	Children-player/Executive
8. I Got It!	Toledo Mud Hens, 5/3 Stadium, Toledo, OH	Minor League ballpark	Frank Gaylord II	23 July 2002	Civic/Individuals	Civic/Individuals	3	Male	White	Children	No	Crowd
9. Who's Up?	Toledo Mud Hens, 5/3 Stadium, Toledo, OH	Minor League ballpark	Emanuel Enriquez	2 September 2002	Civic/Individuals	Civic/Individuals	4	Mixed	Mixed	Children	No	Crowd
10. Joe DiMaggio and child	Joe DiMaggio Hospital, Hollywood, FL	Civic space	Zenos Frudakis	10 October 2002	Individual/Commercial	Individual	1	Male	White	Children	Yes (player)	Children-player/Executive
11. Ted Williams and the Jimmy Fund[d]	JetBlue Park, Fort Myers, FL	Minor League ballpark[c]	Franc Talarico	14 February 2004	Individual	Individual	1	Male	White	Children	Yes (player)	Children-player/Executive
12. Ted Williams and the Jimmy Fund[d]	Boston Red Sox, Fenway Park, Boston, MA	MLB ballpark	Franc Talarico	16 April 2004	Individual	Individual	1	Male	White	Children	Yes (player)	Children-player/Executive

(Continued)

Table 1 – *continued*

Statue	Location	Location type[b]	Sculptor	Date	Promoter	Funder	No. of fans	Gender of fans	Ethnicity of fans	Age of fans	Is specific subject depicted?	Type of statue
13. Stan Musial and fan	Missouri Sports Hall of Fame, Springfield, MO	Museum/Hall of Fame	Harry Weber	2 April 2005	Commercial	Commercial	1	Male	White	Children	Yes (player)	Children-player/Executive
14. Pete Vonachan and fan	Peoria Chiefs, O'Brien Field, Peoria, IL	Minor League ballpark	Lonnie Stewart	4 September 2005	Baseball club	Baseball club	1	Male	White	Children	Yes (executive)	Children-player/Executive
15. The Bryan Bomber	Downtown, Bryan, TX	Civic space	Lynn Haste	22 November 2005	Civic	Civic	2	Mixed	White	Children	No (though includes anonymous player)	Children-player/Executive
16. American Baseball Family Group	Portland Sea Dogs, Hadlock Field, Portland, ME	Minor League ballpark	Rhoda Sherbell	9 April 2007	Baseball club	Baseball club	4	Mixed	White	Mixed (family)	No	Family
17. Brooks Robinson and fans	York Revolution, Sovereign Bank Stadium, York, PA	Minor League ballpark	Lorann Jacobs	5 April 2008	Baseball club	Baseball club	2	Mixed	White	Children	Yes (player)	Children-player/Executive
18. Morrie Silver and fan	Rochester Red Wings, Frontier Field, Rochester, NY	Minor League ballpark	Lyle Johnson	29/06/2008	Baseball club	Baseball club	1	Male	White	Children	Yes (Executive)	Children-player/Executive
19. Joe Nuxhall and children	Waterworks Park, Fairfield, OH	Civic space	Tom Tsuchiya	16 June 2009	Civic	Civic	2	Mixed	White	Children	Yes (player)	Children-player/Executive
20. Rangers Fans (Shannon and Cooper Stone)	Texas Rangers Ballpark, Arlington, TX	MLB ballpark	Bruce Greene	5 April 2012	Baseball club	Baseball club	2	Male	White	Mixed (family)	Yes (fans)	Family
21. Home Run	Winston-Salem Dash, BB&T Field, Winston-Salem, NC	Minor League ballpark	Tom Ogburn	1 April 2014	Sculptor/Civic	Civic/Club individuals	3	Mixed	Mixed	Children	No	Crowd

[a] The statues of Jackie Robinson and children are almost identical in design, the Daytona statue being a very slightly adjusted casting (uniform detail and angle of Robinson's feet) of the Montreal statue.

[b] Within location type, Minor League is taken to mean both MiLB and 'indie league' ballparks.

[c] When the statue of Robinson was erected at the Olympic Stadium in Montreal, the facility was being used by MLB franchise the Montreal Expos, though it no longer accommodates any baseball club.

[d] The Ted Williams and the Jimmy Fund statues in Boston and Florida are identical in design.

[e] Jet Blue Park is used both as a spring training venue by the MLB Boston Red Sox franchise and as a minor league venue for the Red Sox rookie level farm team, the GCL (Gulf Coast League) Red Sox.

Whilst by no means as frequently sculpted as their playing employees, 25 baseball executives, owners, or benefactors have been similarly honoured for their funding, campaigning, and organizational leadership. Compared to statues of players, executive statues, like fan statues, are proportionately more likely to be found at Minor League than Major League ballparks, a locational bias perhaps explained by the relative transience both of MiLB players (leading to a dearth of playing candidates for depiction at MiLB facilities), and particularly in small town locations, the critical role of an owner in winning and retaining an MiLB franchise for his town or city.[42] Three of these executive statues depict the subject interacting with child fans.

The second element of our fan statue typology is the 'Family' statue, which we define through its portrayal of at least one adult fan and one child fan. Four examples currently exist, each depicting family groups on the way to or from a day at the ballpark. Such artworks share themes with the child-player statues described above, in that they feature children, and also because some family groups have been juxtaposed with anonymous ballplayers. Furthermore, by extending the fan portrayal to a whole family, they foreground and project additional messages.

The final subtype of fan statue depicts a crowd scene. Each of these sculptures can be read as both a series of individual portrayals, but primarily as collective visual compositions that commentate on the wider spectator body. The four crowd scene statues in situ depict a variety of crowd behaviours and degrees of interaction between the anonymous subjects, but are distinguishable from the other fan statue subtypes in their portrayal of a group-focused activity where the bond between the fans is baseball-centric rather than familial.

Case Studies

Children-Player Statue: 'Brooks Robinson and Fans', Unveiled 5 April 2008 at York Revolution, Santander Stadium, York, PA. Sculptor: Lorann Jacobs

A quintessential child-player statue, depicting Brooks Robinson with two young fans, stands in front of Santander Stadium, home of the York Revolution, members of the independent Atlantic League. Brooks Robinson, a storied Hall of Famer renowned for his defensive prowess at third base, played his debut season in professional baseball for the York White Roses in 1955.[43] The Roses, a previous incarnation of professional baseball in York, were a class B farm team of the Orioles franchise that Robinson later served with distinction for a record 23 campaigns, making 2,896 appearances and winning 2 World Series rings.[44] Ironically, given Robinson's comparatively brief sojourn in York, this statue predates two other Robinson monuments now located in Baltimore.[45] The statue's genesis was tied to the construction of York's new ballpark in 2007.[46] York Revolution's ownership group was keen to place a statue at the downtown facility. As the city's most famous baseball alumnus and an investor in the ball club, Robinson was the obvious choice.

The owners chose the design in conjunction with the commissioned sculptor, local artist Lorann Jacobs. Inspiration came in part from a Norman Rockwell painting, 'Gee, Thanks Brooks', created in 1971 to advertise Rawlings baseball gloves and Adirondack bats, and rare example of baseball art in which fans play an active or central role. This painting, which depicts Robinson in front of the grandstand, signing a baseball for a boy leaning over the infield wall (Figure 1), is now privately owned by Brooks Robinson himself (though is normally on-loan to Norman Rockwell exhibitions across the USA), and is frequently reproduced in various forms for the sports memorabilia market.[47] 'Gee,

Figure 1   *Gee, Thanks Brooks*, 1971, artist Norman Rockwell

Thanks Brooks', like many of Rockwell's paintings, carries the trademark aesthetics of an idealized, nostalgia-tinged, American childhood.

However, unlike the ekphrasis (the reinterpretation of a work of art in another artistic format) of the many sport statue designs derived from posed or action photographs, which can often be viewed as a simple exchange of dimensionality for context, the York statue differs markedly from its source material. Robinson is sculpted signing a baseball. A boy and a girl stand before him (Figures 2 and 3). The signed ball most likely belongs to the boy, given that the girl is herself holding a baseball. Robinson has also been recast in a York White Roses uniform as opposed to the Orioles jersey painted by Rockwell.

This statue is an exemplar of four interlinked key themes underpinning the fan statuary: hero worship, 'being there', inclusivity (through projecting accessibility and diversity), and the childlike nature of fandom. Hero worship, an intrinsic part of all statues featuring both a player and fans, is projected here by the two young fans looking up at Robinson with a mix of excitement, eagerness, and awe. In both his pose, facing and leaning towards them, and through his action (i.e. signing the boy's baseball), Robinson is responding and engaging willingly, therefore positing baseball as an inclusive, nonhierarchical world populated by accessible, humble, grounded heroes, and York's ballpark as the place to meet them.

Figure 2 *Brooks Robinson and fans*, 2008, bronze, sculptor: Lorann Jacobs. Statue sited at York Revolution, Santander Stadium, York, PA [photo: Eric Milask ©]

The theme of hero worship is strongly linked to a second narrative, that of attending a live sports event. The encounter depicted, a face-to-face meeting with a hero, is most likely to be experienced when attending the ballpark. The clustering of fan statues at Minor League venues reflects the importance of game day attendance to MiLB and independent league baseball organizations' income streams, as opposed to vicarious 'support' of, and revenue generated by MLB teams via television or other media. In an age

Figure 3 *Brooks Robinson and fans*, 2008, bronze, sculptor: Lorann Jacobs. Statue sited at York Revolution, Santander Stadium, York, PA [photo: Eric Milask ©]

when MLB 'follows the fan' via the Internet, mobile apps, and saturation sports coverage, this statue beseeches the fan to experience baseball in person. These messages are foregrounded by the placement of the figures, which stand on low bases rather than a plinth, promoting and enabling interactivity.[48] Fans can pose and be photographed alongside Brooks Robinson's statue. In doing so, they join the two statuesque fans in worshipping a franchise hero without any vertical or horizontal separation.

This statue also reflects the distinctively inclusive Minor League fan experience, which team owners are seeking to promote. One facet of this is accessibility to players. To this end, the York statue is notably different in design from the two other Brooks Robinson statues that stand in Baltimore, and which are respectively sited within and adjacent to the Orioles' Camden Yards ballpark, a Major League facility. Both Baltimore statues, one of which was funded by fans, and the other by the Orioles' franchise, portray Brooks Robinson in playing action. Robinson is portrayed as a heroic action figure, turning the double play or poised to gobble up another ground ball. Fans are not present in either sculpture. The York statue's adaptation of the image from Rockwell's painting (itself an artwork founded upon a desire to market a product), where Brooks Robinson is a (Major League) player for the Orioles, can be seen as a Minor League club attempting a favourable comparison with the grander yet more segregated Major League game day. To meet their idol at a Major League ballpark, as depicted in 'Gee, Thanks Brooks', a fan would have to reach out from the bleachers to the playing area, defying signs discouraging fans from asking a player for his autograph. The lack of any barrier between the statue's fan and player figures encapsulates and promotes the accessibility offered at Minor League level, with its greater opportunities for children to snag a foul ball or collect an autograph. The benevolent Robinson taking the time to sign autographs for children also highlights the 'Tomorrow's Stars Today' appeal of Minor League baseball, in that 'you may not know the name of the player signing your ball, kid, but it might be the next Brooks Robinson'.

This promotion of baseball – and specifically the Revolution's ballpark – as having an inclusive and welcoming culture, also embraces the concept of diversity. The ideal of a diverse fan base is foregrounded through having both a boy and a girl as sculpted fans, whereas Rockwell's painting focuses on a single boy fan. Advocating and proclaiming diversity through design are evident across the five child-player statue designs that feature multiple children (and indeed the wider fan statuary). Four include fans of both genders, and three are also multiethnic fan groups. In York, a further manipulation of the image and tone from the painting that inspired the statue design comes in the sculptor's illustration of the boy fan. Rockwell painted an athletic child, a putative little-leaguer no doubt drawing inspiration from Robinson's playing skills. Jacobs has rendered her boy as less athletic in frame, posture, and appearance: he is skinny and wears large spectacles. Despite his cap and mitt, he does not fulfil the visual stereotype of youthful sporting promise or prowess.

In this way, the statue of Brooks Robinson and fans opens up watching baseball to demographic groups or individuals without a background in playing the sport, or who might see themselves, or be seen by their peers as outside of the tradition of attending a ballgame. Such a widening of its audience is obviously to the franchise's benefit. Fan statues are typically sited at prominent locations such as stadium gates or external plazas. This is true of stadium-sited sports statues more generally, though perhaps more common at minor league stadia, where the smaller concourses and stadium footprint mitigate against a location inside the gates. Whatever the reason, with the trend towards new ballparks being built in downtown locations, such external placement extends a statue's visibility beyond the limits of the stadium and game day, thus further widening the potential audience that they can attract.

Yet in promoting inclusivity, there is a tension with the accompanying, aforementioned motif of hero worship, which asserts the traditional hierarchy of player/ franchise and fan. The presence and placement of the player and fan figures demarcate the stadium forecourt as a space in which they might meet as equals, but the fan behaviour itself is uncritical and submissive. Thus, a franchise's preferred role for the fan within the baseball landscape (i.e. as an adjunct to the players, an unchallenging subject, and unquestioning customer) is reinforced. This distance is only enhanced by the pre-eminence of National Baseball Hall of Fame inductee and MLB All-Century Team member Brooks Robinson. Perhaps when a subject's place in the pantheon of sporting heroes is unchallenged, this 'frees up' his or her statue as a space to exalt personal qualities, such as generosity and humility, as opposed to having to illustrate playing skills. This in turn taps into a further dimension of hero worship. Sociologist Keith Parry notes that, in addition to athletic skills, to be a true sporting hero an athlete must have 'levels of character and charisma for fans to adhere to them'.[49]

Alongside and related to, though distinct from hero worship, 'being there' and inclusivity is a fourth facet of this statue, which forms a consistent theme across all fan statue types: the disproportionate use of images of children to portray the fans. Children appear in every fan statue, and comprise 65% of the 57 distinct fan images across the 21 statues (and, of the 20 adult fans, 14 appear in a single statue). Whilst acknowledging the relatively minor cost saving (in bronze used) by depicting a child rather than an adult, it is more likely that the bias in the age demographic portrayed results from fan statues being used strategically to project a specific brand ideal as opposed to portraying a reality of fandom. It is also worth noting that, whilst the small sample size and geographic spread of soccer fan statues across several different distinct national and soccer cultures preclude any sort of detailed comparison, the soccer fan statuary is so far a less child-centric subgenre, with less than half of the anonymous fans depicted representing a youthful fan base.

The most obvious such strategy is that of drawing children to the ballpark and making them feel at home. As sportswriter Leonard Koppett notes, 'if you can't keep converting children into fans, you can't stay in business'.[50] Attracting children also has the effect of attracting their parents or guardians. By placing the image of the child fan as a norm within the stadium environment, and developing youthful topophilic impulses towards the ballpark that will encourage return visits, baseball organizations, most noticeably those below Major League level with their dependence on game day attendance, are aiming to do just that. The location of so many child-fan statues at Minor League parks also speaks to the developmental aspect of MiLB amongst fans as well as players, promoting their role in offering youngsters a cheap and local means of acquiring a habit for watching live baseball.

Furthermore, in favouring youthful subjects, fan statues are multivalent: that is, they carry and project multiple messages. In addition to welcoming child fans, they also hold meanings for older fans in a similar way to monuments portraying specific storied players of the past, namely through evoking nostalgia and hence attracting them (and their families) to ballgames. There is a wealth of evidence supporting the efficacy of nostalgia in developing an attachment to a team, organization, or place.[51] Through viewing statues of children at the ballpark, fans are prompted to recall and revisit the personal excitement felt at the ballgames of their childhood, and the added thrill of meeting their idols such as Brooks Robinson – and are then enticed to pass that childhood experience on to their own children. Statues depicting a player and child may evoke a collective nostalgia for a more innocent bygone era, where fans perceived players as accessible, grounded, and located figures.

Other ballpark statues that feature children without the adjacent player may instead aim to evoke happy childhood memories of a trip to the ballpark with family. Similarly, the portrayal of multiple children (as in over half of the entire fan statuary, despite the extra cost involved) adds a further dimension by evoking nostalgia for friendships, companionship, and shared excitement, such as battling to snag a foul ball or home run ('I've Got It' at the MiLB franchise Toledo Mud Hens' Fifth Third Park, and 'Home Run' at the Winston-Salem Dash's BB&T Field) and peeking or sneaking into the stadium without paying ('Who's Up' AKA 'The Knothole Gang' a crowd-type statue, also at Toledo Mud Hens, and shown in Figure 4).[52] In both Toledo statues, the nostalgic element is foregrounded by sculpting the children wearing old-time baseball uniforms or street clothes. Emanuel Enriquez, sculptor of 'Who's Up', said: 'When they see the sculpture, they'll relate baseball to their own childhood. They'll envision themselves at a time when they were that age'.[53] Enriquez' comment raises the issue of fan appreciation and reaction to statues, which, whether considering just fan sculptures or any sports statues, is unresearched and offers a fruitful opportunity for future investigation. Even if fans have been able to forward opinions on subject selection or design, which is rarely the case

Figure 4 *Who's Up?* 2002, bronze, sculptor: Emanuel Enriquez. Statue sited at Toledo Mud Hens, Fifth Third Park, Toledo, OH [photo: Nicole Pavlik, Toledo Mud Hens ©]

unless a statue is publicly funded, they have very limited influence in having a statue removed or altered, and lack official right-to-reply channels. Throughout the many ballpark or civic-instigated statues we have researched across the Sporting Statues Project, we did not find a single example of a franchise or public arts committee attempting to systematically gauge the fans reactions post-unveiling. Fans do not get the platform to 'review' a statue in the same way that an art critic does, with feedback typically limited to the most enthusiastic or outraged via social media and online forums/message boards.

Family Statue: 'The American Baseball Family Group', Unveiled 9 April 2007 at Portland Sea Dogs, Hadlock Field, Portland, Maine. Sculptor: Rhoda Sherbell

The majority of fan statues featuring children do not attempt to reflect a continuity of support for baseball into adulthood, instead focusing upon youthful adulation. However, four examples include children as part of a family group of fans. All place the family on the way to or at a ballpark, as opposed to engaging in active support within the stadium.

An example of the 'family statue' genre is *The American Baseball Family Group* (Figure 5), unveiled in spring 2007 outside Hadlock Field, Portland, Maine, the home park of class AA MiLB franchise the Portland Sea Dogs. It features a family, comprising two adults and two children, of Caucasian descent. The father is waving a handful of tickets aloft, his teenage son wears cap, mitt and clutches a baseball, and the mother is holding an infant girl and her cuddly toy. The boy's cap and shirt, and the father's cap are embellished with Sea Dogs logos, and the toy bear also appears to have been bought from the Sea Dogs' club shop. The father's shirt is emblazoned with a US flag. The figures are affixed to the paving in front of the ballpark, with an adjacent plaque inscribed with the simple epithet 'FOR THE PEOPLE OF PORTLAND'.

The statue, commissioned by the Sea Dogs' owner Daniel Burke, is an example of how monuments can easily become contested objects, as a result of their use by individuals, organizations, or communities seeking to impose their own meanings, opinions, and tastes on a public space. As Gary Osmond identifies, 'one of the key sites of disputation and controversy is the "character" of monuments'.[54] It was for this reason that *The American Baseball Family Group* became a local *cause celebre* prior to its unveiling, due to a dispute over the nature of the artwork between Burke and members of Portland's City

Figure 5 *The American Baseball Family Group*, 2007, bronze, sculptor: Rhoda Sherbell. Statue sited at Portland Sea Dogs, Hadlock Field, Portland, ME [photo: Mark Estes ©]

Council. Portland's public art policy requires new artworks proposed for erection at city-owned facilities, such as Hadlock Field, to first seek approval from a public art committee comprised of art professionals and local artists. The Council then vote based upon the committee's recommendation, and their personal prejudices. Whether due to a lack of awareness of this edict (as claimed), or in an attempt to circumnavigate this ruling, Burke attempted to gift the statue to the city without having sought prior approval for the design. Burke had already paid for the sculpting and casting of the artwork, engaging widely respected sculptor Rhoda Sherbell, whose lengthy figurative portfolio includes a critically acclaimed portrayal of legendary New York Yankees' manager Casey Stengel.[55]

In spring 2006, the almost completed artwork was eventually referred to the public arts committee which, after viewing a photograph of the statue maquette (a small model of the statue), voted overwhelmingly to recommend that the Council decline the gift.[56] This sparked a fierce debate within the local community, based both upon the stated reasons for the recommendation and the merits of the artwork itself.[57] The committee cited City codes on installing public art when justifying its decision, specifically articles pertaining to the portrayal and promotion of diversity, the size and placement of statues, and the (mis)use of art for commercial advertising.[58] The former issue caused the greater controversy, though members of the arts committee stated that they were as concerned about the promotional aspect of a statue featuring 'corporate' logos (i.e. the Sea Dogs logo), a charge that neither Burke nor the Sea Dogs' administration attempted to rebut.[59] Public objections centred on the quality and style of the sculpture itself. Conversely, an online survey of 'nearly 4000' readers of the local website MaineToday.com produced strong support in favour of the statue, perhaps in part a countervailing push against perceived civic political correctness.[60]

This wider public feeling, stoked by the local press coverage, was heeded by City Hall. In April 2006, the Council overruled its own committee's recommendation by voting to accept the statue, which was dedicated just over a year later.[61] Irrespective of *The American Baseball Family Group*'s artistic merit, and acknowledging that some fans and politicians may have attenuated their judgement and principles to placate a benefactor providing professional baseball in their (relatively geographically isolated) city – when discussing the statue, Portland's Mayor noted that 'we are fortunate to have the Sea Dogs in Portland' – the public support and the council's heeding of it suggest that the statue was a popular addition to the ballpark.[62] There have not been any attempts to damage the artwork, nor campaigns to have it removed.

The primary importance of *The American Baseball Family Group* to the Sea Dogs' ownership is in portraying Hadlock Field as a favoured family leisure destination, and Minor League baseball as local and affordable entertainment for all the family. Family groups are a key target market for baseball organizations, particularly Minor League teams looking to maximize game day income, and are therefore an obvious choice when choosing a fan demographic to portray through statuary (hence promoting the Sea Dogs brand to that demographic). Families not only constitute multiple ticket sales in the present, and inherited support into the future, but also the 'pester-power' of the younger fans increases consumption of both food and merchandise. The overt promotion of diversity and inclusivity beyond attracting fans of all ages and both genders is not a primary commercial aspiration in Portland. Both Portland and greater Maine are ethnically homogenous relative to the wider USA, hence there would be little benefit in marketing the Sea Dogs by depicting a multiracial group or non-traditional family unit attending a game.[63] Instead, the role of baseball, particularly Minor League baseball, as the chosen sport of the traditional nuclear family is promoted, a sport that has furry mascots, not cheerleaders, a sport where fans' partisanship revolves around consuming and parading in team's merchandise, as opposed to passionate encouragement from the stands. That none of the family fan statues show the subjects actually watching the game or cheering a hit or strike suggest that franchises acknowledge, and indeed are happy for the game to be a minor diversion from the chat as long as the concession stalls keep trading.

The American Baseball Family Group not only overtly promotes the Sea Dogs brand as family-friendly through the appearance of its constituent figures, but also carries themes of tradition and continuity that will attract adult fans. Despite ignoring the sporting elements of the game day spectacle, this statue portrays baseball as a lifetime passion, progressing chronologically from active to vicarious attachment. Dewey describes this as a:

> train of experience starting from the backyard and stopping off at the schoolyard and the local green or lot before arriving at the ballpark ... where the rider got off as an athlete depended on talent and the time to hone that talent. When he did get off, the no-longer-player found ubiquitous reinforcement for maintaining a fan interest in the game.[64]

This temporal continuity of involvement with baseball across generations, which the franchise will obviously seek to perpetuate since it enhances both current and future attendance through minimizing churn, is foregrounded and encouraged by each figure's attire. The boy is sculpted dressed in and carrying baseball equipment, his fandom rooted in still active sporting participation and a desire to emulate heroes, whereas the father is projected purely as a ticket-brandishing consumer, his only playing-related apparel (a cap) hence marginalized to the realm of popular fashion. Furthermore, attending a baseball game, particularly with children, is still viewed as traditional experience, and almost a rite of passage, in a way that is not replicated by other major US sports, be it for reasons of culture, cost, scheduling, location, and ticket availability. Baseball organizations will naturally use this to their advantage, be it through events such Sons and Fathers and Family Day Promotions, or in commercials (such as the 2012 MLB advert, 'Generations').[65] *The American Baseball Family Group* is an attempt to ossify this tradition using a more permanent format, and in a Minor League scenario.

Crowd Statue: 'The Audience', Installed 1989 at Toronto Blue Jays, Rogers Centre, Toronto. Sculptor: Michael Snow

Statues that acknowledge the group dynamic within and between fans, and the fans' collective interaction with players or the ballpark environment, are distinct from other fan statue subtypes. They are best defined as crowd statues. The apotheosis of such designs in both imagination and realism, admittedly within a limited pool of examples, is *The Audience*, sited outside of the Rogers Centre (formerly the Toronto SkyDome), a multipurpose stadium in downtown Toronto. The primary tenants, and by far the most frequent users of the Rogers Centre, are American League MLB franchise the Toronto Blue Jays, though the venue has and continues to host pop concerts, Canadian football, trade conventions, and a range of other sports and entertainment events.[66] One of just five fan statues at a current Major League ballpark, it is also the only specimen that simultaneously captures multiple aspects of crowd behaviour, and gives precedence to adult rather than child figures.[67]

The Audience was installed in 1989 on completion of the construction of the SkyDome. Acclaimed Toronto-based artist Michael Snow won a civic commission to provide an artwork as part of the stadium development.[68] His successful proposal, as reproduced in his memoirs, was to sculpt 'an audience for the audience ... which is arriving to see events at the stadium'.[69] A diptych (that is, an artwork comprised of two distinct parts presented separately), it consists of two crowd scenes, collectively featuring 15 monumental cartoon-grotesque fans modelled in gold-painted fibreglass. The statue protrudes from specially constructed balconies built into the north-facing side-buttresses of the stadium's east and west concrete frontages (Figures 6 and 7).[70] As intended, *The Audience* gazes down upon fans as they approach the Rogers Centre from either of the downtown approaches.

Two plaques (Figure 8), affixed to the stadium walls below each scene, supplement information pertaining to the sculptor and funders with an outline sketch of the artwork, and give names to each character depicted high above. Snow's intention was for positive and negative crowd reactions to be displayed and act as counterpoints.[71] The fans are pictured indulging a range of stereotypical behaviours that he selected after performing a prior survey of audience expressions.[72] Snow describes his fans as those watching the audience arriving for a 'sporting event', but his reference to one of the figures giving a 'kill-the-umpire' reaction suggests a degree of baseball specificity.[73] Numerous behaviours are portrayed and named on the plaques. A camera-happy fan (named 'CAMERA-MAN') has his finger on the button; 'FATSO', a gluttonous fan, with his pot-belly protruding over the balcony, munches upon a hot dog and cradles a supersized drink; an excited child is raised upon his father's shoulders ('MAN AND BOY'), whilst an adjacent fan, 'NOSE THUMBER', expresses derision at the players' performance. 'V

Figure 6 *The Audience*, 1989, painted fibreglass, artist: Michael Snow. Statue sited at Toronto Blue Jays, Rogers Center, Toronto [photo: Christopher Stride ©]

Figure 7 *The Audience*, 1989, painted fibreglass, artist: Michael Snow. Statue sited at Toronto Blue Jays, Rogers Center, Toronto [photo: Christopher Stride ©]

FOR VICTORY' celebrates success with a two-fingered gesture. Next to him, a fan named 'OH NO!' recoils in horror at an outfield blooper or chaos on the base-paths. Thus, fans or passers-by viewing the statues will form their own interpretations of each figure depending on their background and experiences of fandom and sport – but the more curious or unhurried who read the plaques are also steered towards specific meanings. As Gary Osmond states 'Plaques are intended to commemorate and explain, but also to direct audiences'.[74]

The Audience is unique in foregrounding the theme of the fans plural, and also through portraying personal and collective fandom as a role engendering active participation and

Figure 8 *The Audience*, 1989, painted fibreglass, artist: Michael Snow. Statue sited at Toronto Blue Jays, Rogers Center, Toronto [photo: Christopher Stride ©]

emotional commitment with fluctuating feelings and symptoms, some of which may not be consistently pleasurable to the fan nor to those around him, but in which the lows experienced give context to the high points. Snow's crowd scenes are the antithesis of the anodyne, folksy, or sentimental images that characterize the other fan statue types (or to an extent, the other more child-centric crowd statues). This divergence is also undoubtedly linked to a further singular attribute of crowd statues, namely their instigation and funding, which is civic or sculptor-based, unlike the child fan and family statues, which are typically commissioned by baseball organizations. Freed from the artistic restrictions conferred by the marketing strategies and commercial imperatives that propagate franchise-funded art projects, Snow has eschewed the stereotypical image of a player in favour of a fan statue, and further re-envisaged crowd scenes and behaviours that a baseball franchise and stadium ownership might seek to veil, such as opprobrium for the players' performance, and excessive consumption of alcohol.

There were two other factors that made a fan statue of any type a logical choice: the recency of the Toronto franchise and the venue's purpose. The former minimized the field of storied performers to depict at the time of statue's commissioning (the Blue Jays subsequently won two World Series in the early 1990s). In 1989, the lack of a deep or successful baseball tradition in Toronto would also have mitigated against a sentimental, nostalgic image evoking fond memories of childhood ballgame attendance. In fact, the multiuse nature of the SkyDome would have made any overtly baseball-specific statue, such as a specific or even anonymous player hitting or pitching, less appropriate. Paradoxically, despite a non-realist *modus operandi* unique amongst the forest of traditional figurative sculpture found at ballparks, *The Audience* rejects idealism for realism in its narrative, trading romanticized uni-dimensionality for the richness of humanity in all its forms. The caricatured facial profiles uncannily mirror the baseball crowd described by newspaper owner and editor George Wilkes in his sports broadsheet 'The Spirit of the Times' over a century before: ' ... men of all grades, ages, and standing – the young and strong, the aged and feeble, crippled, blind and maimed; garrulous, patient, enthusiastic, combatible and non-combatible, in truth a motley group comprising everything'.[75] It forms an organic group of distinct individuals – all different but together, a collective in which anyone is welcome, yet the antithesis of the homogenous family scene, or any specific organizational ideal for their fan base.

Ambivalence towards presenting a stereotypically attractive image to attract fans is not confined to the statue's individual characters. In its combination of artistic form and elevated location on the stadium walls, *The Audience* strongly resembles the gargoyles, chimeras, and grotesques that adorn medieval European cathedrals, placed there to ward away evil spirits. *The Audience* imagines the crowd as a source of spectacle distinct from and above the ballgame; the ballpark as a *theatre* of the grotesque accommodating a collective mass of humanity that forms a carnival scene, one that is entertaining but also edgily partisan, frightening yet alluring. Yet, through the stylistic choice of cartoonish caricatures, the edge is also taken off crowd behaviours that, if depicted in a strictly realist light, might seem entirely unattractive. Instead, the caricatured images foreground the humour found in conduct considered socially unacceptable in most other settings, but which can act to forge fan camaraderie and provide sideshow entertainment in the context of a ballgame.

Considering the positioning and arrangement of a statue is critical to unlocking its meaning. Butterfield identifies two types of sites where statues are often found.[76] The first is 'along major thoroughfares, so that the greatest number of people can see them and remember the persons whom they commemorate ... the other typical site for a monument is a space of some kind that has been clearly demarcated and set off from the world at large'.[77] Butterfield notes that 'the latter location serves to provide common ground ... where individuals can go to experience membership, to re-establish their identity as parts of a special and distinct social body'.[78] *The Audience*, positioned on a major pedestrian access point to the ballpark, falls primarily into the former category, though large numbers of visitors are only likely to pass on game days or other Rogers Centre events, making its location one that is largely associated with identifiable communities of visitors (albeit not to the statue itself) as opposed to passers-by. Snow claims to have envisaged his 'audience' as viewing their fellow spectators, a dual interpretation encompassing both the real crowd passing below the statue, and a fantasy scene inside the stadium. Both readings acknowledge that fans are often watching, feeding off, and are most entertained by each other. Nonetheless, his figures are most obviously interpreted by the hordes of approaching Blue Jays fans as representations of a baseball crowd.

Statues gain an air of dignity, prominence, and even omnipotence through being fixed upon a raised plinth, though the recent trend for statues of heroic players is for ground-level placement that encourages fan interaction. *The Audience* takes this metaphor for the power balance between fans and players a stage further into what might be seen as role reversal, raising the viewers above the participants. Furthermore, the elevation of *The Audience* is far greater than that provided by a plinth. This reflects both the physical elevation that fans will have within the multitiered stadium, and creates a sense of the fans looking down as masters and judges of their bat and ball gladiators, emphasizing the power of the crowd's collective support or negative reaction in boosting or breaking a player.

Yet through the location of the statue, in their small concrete boxes high on the stadium walls, the crowd figures themselves are also portrayed as trapped – perhaps by their own commitment, which has reached the level at which the team's disappointments become their own. This chimes with the work of sociologist Amir Ben Porat, who considers the sports fan to be voluntarily 'enslaved'; likewise Matthew Klugman writes of the 'agony and suffering' experienced by fans who not only love their team but have taken on a second love, that of the team's desire for success.[79] With some faces contorted with rage and frustration but others displaying joy and excitement, *The Audience* acknowledges this devotion, the consequential behaviour arising from the team's variable success in rewarding it, and the excitement generated by this very uncertainty. As Leonard Koppett has put it, 'The caring ... is the entertainment'.[80] Encouraging or 'teaching' such partisanship might have been appropriate given the reputedly sterile game day atmosphere in the Blue Jays' early seasons as an expansion franchise seeking to establish itself in a location lacking a deeply embedded baseball culture. Dewey comments that 'Blue Jays' players could have done without the polite applause Toronto fans conferred on just about anybody for anything at all (hits by opponents, outs by home team) after the club joined the American League in 1977'.[81]

Though of civic origin, and devoid of Blue Jays branding, *The Audience* is an integral part of the stadium, both through physical attachment to the structure and its provision of visual identity. In this latter respect it benefits the Blue Jays franchise even though the franchise did not commission it. Its elevation and size ensure that, whether sighted from the stadium concourse, or glimpsed from further afield, *The Audience* confers a much-needed motif on to the monotone Rogers Centre. The stadium, smothered on one side by a vast hotel frontage and offering a brutalist concrete exterior, resembles a conference centre more than a sporting venue, and faces strong competition for the passing gaze and 'leisure dollar' from the adjacent CN Tower and other downtown attractions.

Imaging Fan Ideals and the Ideal Fan

Figurative statues typically provide an idealized image. This is as true for sports sculpture as for any other subject-defined figurative genre, with the statues of home-run-hitting or fastball-hurling players that bristle around a Major League ballpark more hagiographic than biographic. Likewise, just as statues depict the hitter striking a rare 'clutch' home run rather than enduring the more frequent swing and a miss, the fan statue will tend to foreground ephemeral highlights or positive aspects of the fan experience. Such idealism is a product of their conception and funding by sports organizations naturally eager to promote what they perceive as the most positive and memorable aspects and experiences of fandom as the norm, within the modern 'hyperreal' ballpark environment that blends fantasy and folksy elements.[82] Furthermore, the design of the typical fan statue unites perceived experiential fan ideals, imaged through the scene depicted, with the commissioner's ideal fans, primarily represented by the demography of the subjects within the scenes.

The thematic decomposition of the fan statuary above reveals these perceived fan ideals to revolve around hero worship of players; a related nostalgic reversion to childlike fandom; a sense of inclusion within a community and of 'being there'; and sharing these pleasurable experiences with family and friends. When constructing their ideal fan, ball clubs, more specifically the Minor League organizations, where the majority of fan statues are sited, treasure children, seeking to position them as a customer with a love of baseball passed down through the generations of a family unit, and, where commercially advantageous, as likely to be female or from a minority ethnic group. A statue enables baseball franchises to place fans displaying such behavioural and demographic exemplars within the crowd in a way that is impossible with a two-dimensional image, and simultaneously be seen to be honouring their game day fans, so crucial to the economics of Minor League baseball, in a manner equal to that conferred upon players at MLB ballparks.

The ideal fan, and hence fan statue design, is framed by both contemporary values and a commercial imperative. Children make up two-thirds of statue figures and appear in all statues. A cursory glance around an MLB or Minor League ballpark would indicate that this comfortably exceeds the proportion of ticket sales to under-18s, even in weekend matinee games.

The extent to which crowd gender and ethnicity profiles are representative is less clear. Though neither MLB nor MiLB organizations track the ethnic or gender balance of their fans, independent surveys from between 1999 and 2010 suggested ethnic minorities formed just over 20% of fans (divided roughly equally between African-American and Hispanic fans), though not every study considered fandom in terms of game day attendance. More detailed statistics indicated that Afro-Americans were both under-represented (given the demographics of cities with MLB teams) and decreasingly likely to attend games, though the MLB fan base ethnicity profile resembled that of the US population.[83] A 2012 market research report claimed that 46% of self-identified baseball fans were female, with previous research finding slightly lower but similar figures (though this does not necessarily reflect actual attendance, a 2009 Minor League game day survey placed the female fan percentage at 31%).[84] Of the 57 fan statue figures, 24% appear to be female and 12% are sculpted with facial characteristics and hairstyles that would suggest they are Afro-American; just one fan possibly has Hispanic features.

At first glance, these figures indicate an under-representation of women and particularly Hispanic fans in the statuary. However, in the 12 statues where multiple children are depicted together, all but one group is mixed in one or both of gender and/or ethnicity. Furthermore, specific examples support the promotion of diversity, such as the adaptation of Rockwell's entirely masculine 'Gee, Thanks Brooks' into a statue that also features a girl. Hence, fan statues are likely to offer a skewed portrayal of fan group composition: one that overtly promotes the ballpark as a racially harmonious and gender-balanced family environment.

A degree of what might be termed 'political correctness' in statue images is entirely predictable and understandable. An accurate description of the national fan demographic is unlikely to be even a minor priority for either ball clubs or sculptors. Baseball organizations will aspire to maintain and grow their fan base in the way they deem most effective. Hence, they will want to provide an image that will entice and welcome old and new fans, and promote positive public relations (though they may also be subject to local public art policy strictures regarding representation). Sculptors will seek to provide an artwork that simultaneously satisfies their client's commission, enhances their reputation, and, if possible, fulfils their inherent desire to create. When a ballpark is situated downtown, as many of the recently constructed facilities are, and the statue is located on the periphery of the stadium, a fan statue markets the fan ideal *and* the ideal fan to passers-by. Research shows baseball's audience to be aging, and a reduction in youth participation. Commentators have expressed concern over the longer-term implications of this in terms of merchandise sales, advertising revenues and game day attendances (especially given the perceived increased competition from soccer), and the decline in Afro-Americans playing baseball at both elite and junior levels.[85] Given the increasing diversity of the US population as a whole, appealing to minority groups has become increasingly important to all sports organizations.[86] On the other hand, Hispanic engagement with baseball has increased in line with their increasing representation on the field, so it may not be seen as a priority to promote to this particular group.[87] The promotion of baseball to female fans via fan statuary carries a further dimension in that subject-specific statues of famous past players are exclusively male; hence, fan statues represent the only female 'characters' throughout the baseball statuary (other than a single statue of an anonymous female baseball player at the National Baseball Hall of Fame Museum [NBHOF]).

Nevertheless, the detail within the portrayals of fandom suggests that, if gender diversity in particular is being promoted, there is a degree of superficiality in the message projected. For example, a closer inspection of multi-gender statue groups reveals the boys depicted as more likely to be 'interacting with baseball' than girls, be it in their wearing of baseball apparel, or their physical adjacency to a famous player. In *The American Baseball Family Group*, only the father and son wear branded clothing; in the statue of Brooks Robinson and fans, it is the boy who is getting his baseball signed; in 'Who's Up', the boys lead the way in peeping into the ballpark. Furthermore, whenever a fan statue contains just a single child, that child is male. Ultimately, if a gender-related design choice has had to be made, the commissioners and sculptors have retreated to a stereotype of male fandom and participation. Therefore, these fan statue designs reflect the inherent tension and resultant compromise between, on one hand, a political need and commercial imperative of promoting modern values such as diversity and inclusivity, and on the other, traditional views of fandom or a desire to evoke nostalgia that involves depicting a less diverse past.

If clubs are creating fan statues to attract (and retain) fans, it is worth considering whether the designs that they have commissioned, or an alternative vision of crowd behaviour and demography, would best fulfil these aims. The fan statuary not only seeks to attract child fans through expectation of the idealized experience depicted, and their elders through reminisce and nostalgia, but also casts fandom as a fundamentally childlike state. Childlike fandom, in its inherent subjugation to the sports organization, partisan and unblinking support irrespective of the team's performance, and unthinking consumption of food and drink, is a convenient state for sports organizations to feed, control, and profit from: in these aspects it represents the ideal fan (state). Encouraging these fan behaviours through facility enhancement is not limited to the erection of stimuli such as statues. It can also be seen in the provision of escapist, essentially childlike diversions within the interior of new ballparks, such as swimming pools, video games, all you can eat buffet terraces, and promotional events such as ex-Major Leaguers signing autographs or bobblehead toy giveaways – essentially creating a baseball-styled theme park.[88] The attraction of childlike fandom to all ages is observed in the queue of autograph hunters at the signing tent, the multimillion dollar business built around the trading of baseball cards, and the ageless fight for the foul ball. The majority of those involved in these activities, especially at MLB ballparks, are not children or family groups, but adults. It is these innocent childlike features of fandom that the ball club wants to promote, hence pitching the ballpark as a place where you can become a child again.

The Crowd: A Marginalized Attraction

Nonetheless, such fan statues describe only a partial constituent of the baseball experience and audience. Childlike fandom and hero worship, at least as depicted in fan statues, are not narratives that will appeal to every fan, even if those same fans' behaviour may often be considered childlike. Through their uni-dimensional message, fan statues may become monuments to exclusion as well as inclusion. Though such exclusion is highly unlikely to be a ball club's primary intent when commissioning a specific design, it is also possible that sports organizations recognize but simply do not wish to acknowledge the full range of fan cultures and motivations that exist in their ballpark, the crowd as an amorphous body distinct from the individual (ideal) fan, or, in some respects, the fan as distinct from the spectator or customer. As Dewey opines,

> The sport has only reluctantly left to disinterested eyes the characterisation of its own fans ... in the official version the rowdies, gamblers and drunks glimpsed in the lower decks have been as endemic to baseball as Fatty Arbuckle was to Hollywood: unfortunate aberrations and ugliness rooted to eras long since overcome.[89]

Such a bias would explain the preference of baseball franchises for depicting the fan, as opposed to the fans, when creating statuary. The individual fan is unlikely to compete with the players to be the centre of attention, and in singular form carries minimal threat to the control that a sports organization exerts over its image and stadium environment. On the other hand, the crowd is a vast, amorphous body with the potential not only to provide support for the team and enhance the spectacle, but also to deliberately or unintentionally make its own entertainment, and even offer disagreement, opposition, or downright revolt that has on occasions proved impossible to manage.[90] Therefore, a ball club may feel reluctant to remind the crowd of its collective power through statuary. Yet, by limiting their palette in this way, they also ignore the crowd's potential allure.

The Audience, a civic-funded statue, may be a more effective tool than the anodyne fan statues found elsewhere in attracting fans both young and old, albeit within the different context of MLB as opposed to MiLB. Ironically, it mirrors themes which the more orthodox or idealistic fan portrayals wish to project, such as a sense of community, fandom as escapism, and behaviour that is truly childlike. However, it achieves this through a lens un-tinted by a desire to promote behavioural conformity or traditional family values. Where *The American Baseball Family Group* posits baseball as a vicarious leisure activity to be enjoyed with an external family (i.e. the family comes to baseball for casual entertainment, with collective commitment pitched somewhere between spectator and fan), *The Audience* offers the ballgame as an all-consuming passion, and its attendant community as an alternative family, one that the fan can become part of. This offering is of far greater depth and commitment, and will provide a range of emotions, both positive and negative. Contiguous to this multivalent message, the grotesque styling of *The Audience*'s imagery both repels and entices. As well as being promoting the Rogers Centre as a setting for feats of sporting prowess that stir positive emotions, *The Audience* markets the ballpark as a venue for a darker tourism, where the good times may be outweighed by the disappointments, or even where amusement may be found in witnessing the suffering of others.[91] The greater commitment portrayed and demanded, and the varying shades and tones of emotional attachment that *The Audience* depicts may offer greater appeal to some prospective and current fans, though draw a stronger negative reaction from others.

Statues of baseball players proliferate across North America, but, especially where the player is depicted in action, they are analogous to cropped photographs, in which the crowd, and the context that it brings to the image, has been removed from the spectacle. The 'fan-scape' forms an essential part of the spectacle of live sport, both providing a market to finance it and a backdrop for it that, through its colour, atmosphere, and behaviour, offers a diversionary and on occasion primary source of entertainment. Therefore, the fans' depiction in bronze, either alongside statues of players or alone, may be seen as a rightful reinstatement within the game day montage. Yet, in their portrayal, the collective fan body and much of its character has been marginalized.

Each fan statue shares a common thread: imaging the extra-dimension that personal experience brings to a fan's enjoyment of their sport. Through their placement within a stadium environment, authentic fandom is equated with physical presence. Conversely, to the committed fan, part of what this statuary depicts would appear deeply inauthentic, consisting of ephemeral or once-in-a-lifetime brushes with fame, or idealized beyond recognition. This is partly due to a focus upon, and resulting limitations imposed through depicting the fan singular. A single fan's visage, or even the family or friendship group's collective expressions, will always fail to reflect the gamut of emotions associated with strong allegiance to a sports team. But this bronzed evocation of fandom is further distorted by the commercial imperative that has motivated much of it – a one-dimensional branding strategy resulting in the strong similarities shared by these multidimensional images.

Fan statues exist largely due to sports organizations' desire to enhance current and prospective fans' team identification, leading to deeper attachment and subsequent loyalty. A statue's visibility, capacity to hold and project multiple meanings, and depict perceived fan ideals of different generations of 'ideal fans', has made it an increasing popular addition to the ballpark environs, its permanence complementing the ephemeral game day promotions. However, by being focused on 'ideal fans' and perceived fan ideals, the typical sports organization-commissioned fan statue projects a limited selection of the drivers in the creation and embedding of fandom. The motivations of group affiliation, eustress, and escape are being largely forgotten or ignored. We argue that it would be beneficial for both clubs and for the accurate representation of game day if any future fan statues followed the *The Audience*'s lead and portrayed the fan experience by putting 'the fans' back into the depiction of 'the fan'.

Underlying Research Materials

The underlying research materials for this article can be accessed at the Sporting Statues Project website at http://www.sportingstatues.com

Disclosure statement

No potential conflict of interest was reported by the authors.

Notes

1. Susanna M. Ekholm, 'Ceramic Figurines and the Mesoamerican Ballgame', in Vernon Scarborough and David R. Wilcox (eds), *The Mesoamerican Ballgame* (Tucson: University of Arizona Press, 1991), 241–9; Stephen G. Miller, *Ancient Greek Athletics* (New Haven, CT: Yale University Press, 2004); and Ian Jenkins, *The Discobolus* (London: The British Museum Press, 2012).
2. Between January 2011 and March 2014, the first and second authors constructed a series of databases of existing and planned statues of sportsmen and women around the world as part of a wider project into commemoration in sport. Four specific databases focus on: UK-sited statues of all sportsmen and women; North American-sited statues of baseball players, managers, broadcasters, executives, and fans; statues of cricketers and cricket umpires anywhere in the world; and statues of soccer players, managers, chairmen, administrators, and fans anywhere in the world. Data and images were obtained through a literature, archival, and online search, and via interviews with sculptors and project organizers. Variables collected included the precise location, date of unveiling, design type (broadly classified as 'action', 'posed', or 'triumph'), the full plaque or plinth inscription, and the identity of the statue project promoters and funders, as well as further demographic and performance information on the subjects depicted. Each database is complete and accurate to the best of our knowledge, and publicly available via the project website at http://www.sportingstatues.com.
3. Ibid. The baseball database was completed and launched online in March 2013. Prior to its launch, baseball historians from a national spread of chapters of the Society for American Baseball Research (SABR) and the NBHOF were invited to view the draft version and suggest any omissions or errors. In the month following its launch, the website received over 10,000 unique visitors and substantial regional and national press coverage across North America, yet only one further subject-specific statue erected prior to March 2013 was discovered added as a result of information received after the launch. The authors have continued to maintain and update the database with information drawn from through frequent online searches and contacts within the sports sculpture industry.
4. A small number of figurative statues featuring soccer fans have recently been unveiled at football stadia: specifically at Sunderland FC and Dartford FC (UK), Real Betis, RCD Espanyol, Valencia CF, and Granada CF (Spain), FC Tom Tomsk (Russia), and the Azteca

Stadium in Mexico City. See Christopher Stride, Ffion E. Thomas, and John Wilson, 'The Sporting Statues Project', http://www.sportingstatues.com, for details of each statue.

5. Ibid.

6. Mike Huggins, 'Death, Memorialisation and the Victorian Sporting Hero', *The Local Historian* 38, no. 4 (2008), 257–65; Mike McGuinness, 'The Canonisation of Common People: Memorialisation and Commemoration in Football', in Jeffrey Hill, Kevin Moore, and Jason Wood (eds), *Sport, History, and Heritage: Studies in Public Representation* (Woodbridge: Boydell Press, 2012), 211–22; Gary Osmond, 'Shaping Lives: Statues as Biography', *Sporting Traditions* 27, no. 2 (2010), 101–11; Gary Osmond, Murray G. Phillips, and Mark O'Neill, '"Putting Up Your Dukes": Statues Social Memory and Duke Paoa Kahanamoku', *The International Journal of the History of Sport* 23, no. 1 (2006), 82–103; Maureen M. Smith, 'Frozen Fists in Speed City: The Statue as Twenty-First-Century Reparations', *Journal of Sport History* 36, no. 3 (2009), 393–414; Maureen M. Smith, 'Mapping America's Sporting Landscape: A Case Study of Three Statues', *The International Journal of the History of Sport* 28, nos 8–9 (2011), 1252–68; and Christopher Stride, John Wilson, and Ffion E. Thomas, 'Honouring Heroes by Branding in Bronze', *Sport in Society* 16, no. 6 (2013), 749–71.

7. Mike O'Mahony and Mike Huggins (eds), 'The Visual in Sport (Prologue)', in *The Visual in Sport* (London: Routledge, 2011), 6.

8. Kirk Savage, 'The Politics of Memory: Black Emancipation and the Civil War Monument', in J.R. Gillis (ed.), *Commemorations: The Politics of National Identity* (Princeton, NJ: Princeton University Press, 1994), 135; Judith Dupre, *Monuments: America's History in Art and Memory* (New York: Random House, 2007), 7.

9. The only statue to depict specific fans portrays Shannon Stone, a Texas Rangers fan who fell to his death from an upper tier of the Rangers ballpark in July 2011 when attempting to catch a foul ball tossed into the crowd. He is depicted alongside his young son. See R. Durrett, 'Rangers Unveil Statue of Fan', *ESPN*, http://espn.go.com/dallas/mlb/story/_/id/7780391/texas-rangers-unveil-statue-fan-died-game (accessed 11 August 2014).

10. Osmond, Phillips, and O'Neill, 'Putting Up Your Dukes'; Smith, 'Frozen Fists in Speed City'; Stride, Wilson, and Thomas, 'Honouring Heroes by Branding in Bronze'; George Ritzer and Todd Stillman, 'The Postmodern Ballpark as a Leisure Setting: Enchantment and Simulated De-Mcdonaldization', *Leisure Sciences* 23 (2001), 99–113; Chad Seifried and Katherine Meyer, 'Nostalgia-Related Aspects of Professional Sports Facilities: A Facility Audit of Major League Baseball and National Football League Strategies to Evoke the Past', *International Journal of Sport Management Recreation and Tourism* 5 (2010), 51–76.

11. Smith, 'Mapping America's Sporting Landscape'.

12. Allen Guttmann, *Sport and American Art from Benjamin West to Andy Warhol* (Amherst: University of Massachusetts Press, 2011), 162.

13. Ibid., Plate 25, 163.

14. Examples of ballpark murals featuring fans include a stadium scene at Citizen's Bank park, Philadelphia (see Margaret Almon, 'Phillies in Mosaic: Jonathan Mandell', *Margaret Almon Mosaics*, http://www.margaretalmon.com/phillies-in-mosaic-jonathan-mandell/ [accessed 26 March 2015]), and 'A History of Minnesota Baseball' at Target Field, Minneapolis (see Craig David, 'Cut-Stone Murals', *Art davidii*, http://www.artdavidii.com/cut-stone.html [accessed 26 March 2015]). An older example of a baseball mural is the Public Works of Art Project-funded piece painted in 1934 at Norwalk City Hall, Connecticut (see *The Living New Deal*, 'Norwalk City Hall: Avison Murals – Norwalk CT', http://livingnewdeal.org/projects/norwalk-city-hall-avison-murals-norwalk-ct/ [accessed 26 March 2015]).

15. Daniel L. Wann, *Sport Psychology* (Upper Saddle River, NJ: Prentice Hall, 1997), 346.

16. Daniel L. Wann et al., *Sports Fans: The Psychology and Social Impact of Spectators* (New York: Routledge, 2001), 2.

17. Fred Stein, *A History of the Baseball Fan* (Jefferson, NC: McFarland, 2005), 2.

18. For an extensive review of the fan motivation literature, see Walter Gantz et al., 'Exploring the Roots of Sports Fanship', in L. Hugenberg, P.M. Haridakis, and A.C. Earnheardt (eds), *Sports Mania: Essays on Fandom and the Media in the 21st Century* (Jefferson, NC: McFarland, 2008), 63–78.

19. Wann, *Sport Psychology*, 329–31; Wann et al., *Sports Fans*, 31–42.

20. Wann et al., *Sports Fans*, 62; Daniel L. Wann and Paula J. Waddill, 'Predicting Sport Fan Motivation Using Anatomical Sex and Gender Role Orientation', *North American Journal of*

Psychology 5 (2003), 485–98; and Matthew Klugman, 'Loves, Suffering and Identification: The Passions of Australian Football League Fans', *The International Journal of the History of Sport* 26, no. 1 (2009), 21–44.

21. Daniel C. Funk and Jeff James, 'Consumer Loyalty: The Meaning of Attachment in the Development of Sport Team Allegiance', *Journal of Sport Management* 20, no. 2 (2006), 189–217.
22. Ibid.
23. Wann et al., *Sports Fans*, 59.
24. Ibid, 60.
25. Stein, *History of the Baseball Fan*, 32.
26. mlb.com, 'Mlb Finishes 2013 with Sixth Best Attendance Total Ever: Last Decade Includes 10 Best-Attended Individual Seasons in Mlb History', http://mlb.mlb.com/news/article.jsp?ymd=20131001&content_id=62282120&vkey=pr_mlb&c_id=mlb (accessed 7 May 2014).
27. Stein, *History of the Baseball Fan*, 33.
28. Jeff James and Stephen Ross, 'The Motives of Sport Consumers: A Comparison of Major and Minor League Baseball', *International Journal of Sport Management* 3, no. 3 (2002), 180–98.
29. Ken Burns and Lynn Novick, *Baseball: A Film by Ken Burns, the First Inning: Our Game* (City: PBS Home Video, 1994), Film.
30. Matthew Bernthal and Peter Graham, 'The Effect of Sport Setting on Fan Attendance Motivation: The Case of Minor League vs Collegiate Baseball', *Journal of Sport Behavior* 26, no. 3 (2003), 223–40; Amber L. Rickard, Frederick G. Grieve, and W. Pitt Derryberry, 'Motivational Profiles of Sports Fan Attending Different Levels of Baseball Games', in J.H. Humphrey (ed.), *Contemporary Athletics Compendium*, vol. 3 (Hauppauge, NY: Nova Science, 2009), 26; and Stephen Ross and Jeff James, 'Major versus Minor League Baseball: The Relative Importance of Factors Influencing Spectator Attendance', *International Journal of Sport Management* 7, no. 2 (2006), 217–33.
31. Mark McDonald and Daniel Rascher, 'Does Bat Day Make Cents? The Effect of Promotions on the Demand for Major League Baseball', *Journal of Sport Management* 14 (2000), 8–17.
32. Ibid.
33. Larry Bortstein. 'Minor Leagues, Major Fun', *Sports Travel Magazine* 12, no. 2 (2008), 26.
34. Thomas K. Hixson, 'Price and Non-Price Promotions in Minor League Baseball and the Watering Down Effect', in *The Sport Journal* (United States Sports Academy, 2008), http://thesportjournal.org/article/price-and-non-price-promotions-in-minor-league-baseball-and-the-watering-down-effect/ (accessed 7 March 2014).
35. Owen Covington, 'With New Statue, Jim Melvin Expands Mark on Newbridge Bank Park', *Triad Business Journal*, 2014, http://www.bizjournals.com/triad/blog/2014/06/with-new-statue-jim-melvin-expands-mark-on.html (accessed 17 August 2014).
36. Ross and James, 'Major versus Minor League Baseball', 26; Scott E. Branvold, David W. Pan, and Trent E. Gabert, 'Effects of Winning Percentage and Market Size on Attendance in Minor League', *Sport Marketing Quarterly* 6, no. 3 (1997), 32; and Cindy Lee and Doyeon Won, 'Understanding Segmented Spectator Markets of a Minor League Baseball (Milb) Team', *Event Management* 16 (2012), 352.
37. John Feinstein, *Where Nobody Knows Your Name: Life in the Minor Leagues of Baseball* (New York: Doubleday Books, 2014). See also Dirk Hayhurst, *The Bullpen Gospels: Major League Dreams of a Minor League Veteran* (New York: Citadel Press, 2010). Feinstein provides several examples of former MLB players, several of whom won major MLB awards or were involved in famous moments or games, who are attempting comebacks in MiLB but who receive little recognition from spectators at MiLB ballparks. The memoirs of pitcher Dirk Hayhurst provide a more personal perspective on the same experience.
38. Donald Dewey, *The 10th Man: The Fan in Baseball History* (New York: Carroll & Graf, 2004), xvii.
39. Ibid, xi.
40. Stride, Thomas, and Wilson, 'The Sporting Statues Project'.
41. Of the six real players depicted alongside fans, 5 (Brooks Robinson, Jackie Robinson, Stan Musial, Joe DiMaggio, and Ted Williams) were amongst just 30 players selected to the MLB's twentieth century 'All Century Team' in 1999. See Baseball Almanac, 'All Century Team', http://www.baseball-almanac.com/legendary/limc100.shtml (accessed 11 May 2014).
42. Of the 25 statues of pioneers, executives or administrators, 40% are found at Minor League ballparks, compared to 10% of all player statues.

43. Rick Wolff, *Brooks Robinson* (New York: Chelsea House, 1991), 21; Bob Kuenster, 'All-Time Best Third Basemen Starred as Hitters, Fielders', *Baseball Digest* 53, no. 9 (1994), 32–8.

44. Wolff, *Brooks Robinson*; Baseball Reference, 'Brooks Robinson (Minor League Stats)', 2010, 40, http://www.baseball-reference.com/minors/player.cgi?id=robins001bro and http://www.baseball-reference.com/players/r/robinbr01.shtml (accessed 13 June 2014).

45. Judy DePauw, 'Brooks Robinson Statue', The Babe Ruth Birthplace Foundation, Inc., http://www.brooksrobinsonstatue.org/home (accessed 10 May 2014); Childs Walker, 'Brooks Robinson Rebounding from Health Scares, Excited for Sculpture Unveiling', *The Baltimore Sun*, http://articles.baltimoresun.com/2012-09-28/sports/bs-sp-orioles-brooks-statue-20120928_1_brooks-robinson-frank-robinson-sculpture (accessed 7 May 2014).

46. The ballpark was originally named Sovereign Bank Stadium, with Santander taking over naming rights in 2013.

47. Personal communication by first author with Paul Braverman, curator, York Revolution, 12 November 2012. See also York Revolution, 'Santander Stadium', http://www.yorkrevolution.com/game-day-info/santander-stadium.html (accessed 12 May 2014).

48. Information on Brooks Robinson's career is given via inscribed plaques embedded in the pavement around the statue.

49. Keith D. Parry, 'Search for the Hero: An Investigation into the Sports Heroes of British Sports Fans', *Sport in Society* 12, no. 2 (2009), 223.

50. Leonard Koppett, *Sports Illusion, Sports Reality*, (Boston, MA: Houghton Mifflin, 1981), 221.

51. Funk and James, 'Consumer Loyalty'; Sheranne Fairley, 'In Search of Relived Social Experience: Group-Based Nostalgia Sport Tourism', *Journal of Sport Management* 17, no. 3 (2003), 284–304; Gregory Ramshaw and Sean Gammon, 'More than Just Nostalgia? Exploring the Heritage/Sport Tourism Nexus', *The Journal of Sport Tourism* 10, no. 4 (2005), 229–41; and Vincent J. Pascal, David E. Sprott, and Darrel D. Muehling, 'The Influence of Evoked Nostalgia on Consumers' Responses in Advertising: An Exploratory Study', *Journal of Current Issues and Research in Advertising* 24 (2002), 39–49.

52. Rebekah Scott, 'Hens' New House to Gain $450,000 in Artistic Touches', *The Toledo Blade*, http://www.toledoblade.com/frontpage/2001/10/23/Hens-new-house-to-gain-450-000-in-artistic-touches.html#0dt6gRT3h3KJKYaa.99 (accessed 13 October 2014).

53. D. Dupont, 'At Bat: Enriquez Takes a Swing with Ballpark Figure' (Sentinel-Tribune, Wood County OH, 29 August 2002).

54. Osmond, Phillips, and O'Neill, 'Putting Up Your Dukes', 88.

55. Sculpture Review, 'National Portrait Gallery Chooses Rhoda Sherbell', *Sculpture Review* 45, no. 3 (1997), 32.

56. K. Bouchard, 'City Art Panel Says "No Thanks" to Statues', *Portland Press Herald*, 16 March 2006.

57. Staff Writer, 'Statues a Good Fit for Hadlock Field', *Portland Press Herald*, 17 March 2006.

58. Bouchard, 'City Art Panel Says "No Thanks" to Statues'.

59. The Associated Press, 'Committee Concerned Statues Aren't Diverse', *Bangor Daily News*, 10 March 2006, B8.

60. The Associated Press, 'Portland Council Decides to Accept Sea Dogs Statues', *Bangor Daily News*, 23 March 2006, B6. Public comments on the statues and the council decision can be seen here: AsMaineGoes, 'Portland's Public Art Committee ~ Free Statue Not Diverse', http://www.asmainegoes.com/content/portlands-public-art-committee-free-statue-not-diverse (accessed 11 August 2014).

61. The Associated Press, 'Portland Council Decides to Accept Sea Dogs Statues'; B. Keyes, 'Controversial Art in Place at Hadlock Field', *Portland Press Herald*, 10 April 2007, A1.

62. D. Sharp, 'Disputed Baseball Statue to Be Unveiled Today', *Bangor Daily News*, 9 April 2007, B2.

63. In 2010, the predominant ethnicity of Portland was white (85% of the population), with no single other ethnic group comprising more than 6% of the population. The state of Maine was 95% white. This compares to 71% white, for the USA as a whole. See United States Census Bureau, 'State & County QuickFacts', http://quickfacts.census.gov/qfd/index.html (accessed 11 August 2014).

64. Dewey, *The 10th Man*, 77.

65. Major League Baseball, 'Generations', MLB FanCave, 2012.

66. See, for example, the Rogers Centre calendar of events at http://events.rogerscentre.com/. For August 2014 this listed 15 Blue Jays games, 2 pop concerts by One Direction, 2 Toronto Argonauts (Canadian Football) games, and a charity event to end women's cancer.

67. The other four current Major League ballparks with fan statues are the Chase Field (Arizona Diamondbacks), Progressive Field (Cleveland Indians), Rangers Ballpark (Texas Rangers), and Fenway Park (Boston Red Sox). One of the two statues of Jackie Robinson and fans stands at the Olympic Stadium in Montreal, which was home of the Major League Montreal Expos when the statue was unveiled but no longer hosts baseball at any level. However, this site was a second choice location for Robinson's statue. For more detail on the history of this statue, see Christopher B. Stride, Ffion E. Thomas, and Maureen M. Smith, 'Ballplayer or Barrier Breaker? Branding through the Seven Statues of Jackie Robinson', *The International Journal of the History of Sport* 31, no. 17 (2014), 2164–96.

68. Robert Brehl, 'Skydome Sculptures Will Get Rise Out of Fans', *Toronto Star*, 8 December 1988, C3; Christopher Hume, 'The Audience Pokes Fun at Fans', *Toronto Star*, 23 May 1989.

69. Michael Snow and Louise Dompierre, *The Collected Writings of Michael Snow: The Michael Snow Project* (Waterloo: Wilfrid Laurier University Press, 1994), 253.

70. Rogers Centre Public Relations, 'Art Inspired by Life', Rogers Stadium Limited Partnership, http://www.rogerscentre.com/fun/article.jsp?content=20090715_103535_5412 (accessed 5 February 2014).

71. Snow and Dompierre, *Collected Writings of Michael Snow*, 253.

72. Ibid.

73. Ibid.

74. Osmond, 'Shaping Lives', 104.

75. George Wilkes, 'Wilkes' Spirit of the Times 1868', 6 June 1868; Dewey, *The 10th Man*, 32.

76. Andrew Butterfield, 'Monuments and Memories – What History Can Teach the Architects at Ground Zero', *The New Republic*, 3 February 2003, 27–32, http://www.newrepublic.com/article/monuments-and-memories (accessed 20 March 2015).

77. Ibid., 30.

78. Ibid.

79. Amir Ben-Porat, 'Football Fandom: A Bounded Identification', *Soccer & Society* 11, no. 3 (2010), 280; Klugman, 'Loves, Suffering and Identification', 21.

80. Koppett, *Sports Illusion, Sports Reality*, 15.

81. Dewey, *The 10th Man*, 233.

82. Ritzer and Stillman, 'Postmodern Ballpark', 105.

83. Mark Hyman, 'The Racial Gap in the Grandstands', in *Bloomberg Business Magazine* (Bloomberg L.P., 2006), http://www.businessweek.com/stories/2006-10-01/the-racial-gap-in-the-grandstands (accessed 22 May 2014); Randy Tucker, 'Reds, Baseball Missing Black Fans', in *The Cincinnati Enquirer*, cincinnati.com (Cincinnati, OH: The Cincinnati Enquirer, 2000), http://reds.enquirer.com/2000/07/09/red_reds_baseball.html (accessed 23 May 2014); Dewey, *The 10th Man*, 341; and Sports Business Daily, 'Fan Demographics among Major North American Sports Leagues', in *Sports Business Daily Global Journal*, sportsbusinessdaily.com (American City Business Journals, 2010), http://www.sportsbusinessdaily.com/Daily/Issues/2010/06/Issue-185/The-Back-Of-The-Book/Fan-Demographics-Among-Major-North-American-Sports-Leagues.aspx (accessed 23 May 2014).

84. Sport Business Daily, 'Scarborough Sports Marketing Examines MLB Fan Demographics', in *Sports Business Daily Global Journal*, sportsbusinessdaily.com (American City Business Journals, 2008); Sport Business Daily, 'Fan Demographics among Major North American Sports Leagues', in *Sports Business Daily Global Journal*, sportsbusinessdaily.com (American City Business Journals, 2010), http://www.sportsbusinessdaily.com/Daily/Issues/2010/06/Issue-185/The-Back-Of-The-Book/Fan-Demographics-Among-Major-North-American-Sports-Leagues.aspx (accessed 21 June 2014); Soon Hwan Lee, Timothy J. Newman, and Hyejin Bang, 'Understanding Spectators of Minor League Baseball: Group Differences on External and Internal Factors in Minor League Baseball' (paper presented at the 2009 North American Society for Sport Management Conference, Columbia, SC, 2009); Kelly L. Balfour, 'Life in the Stands: The Experiences of Female Major League Baseball Fans' (PhD thesis, University of Tennessee, Knoxville, 2012); Milwaukee Brewers, 'Demographics', MLB Advanced Media, L.P., http://milwaukee.brewers.mlb.com/mil/sponsorship/demographics/index.jsp (accessed 11 August 2014); and Beth Dietz-Uhler et al., 'Sex Differences in Sport Fan Behavior and Reasons for Being a Sport Fan', *Journal of Sport Behavior* 22, no. 3 (2000), 219–33.

85. Matt Sullivan, 'The Tinturn Abbey Nine: Why Baseball's TV Demographics Aren't a Major Issue', in *MLB Daily Dish*, SB Nation (2014), http://www.mlbdailydish.com/2014/2/15/

5412264/MLB-advance-media-aging-tv-demographics (accessed 11 August 2014); Matthew Futterman, 'Why Kids Aren't Watching Baseball', in *The Wall Street Journal* (New York: The Wall Street Journal, 2013), http://online.wsj.com/news/articles/SB1000142405270230384 3104579167812218839786 (accessed 27 July 2014).

86. U.S. Census Bureau, 'U.S. Census Bureau Projections Show a Slower Growing, Older, More Diverse Nation a Half Century from Now', http://www.census.gov/newsroom/releases/archives/population/cb12-243.html (accessed 12 July 2014).

87. beisbol.net, 'Targeting the Hispanic Baseball Fan', in *Beisbol SBN* (Beisbol SBN, 2009), http://beisbol.net/wp-content/uploads/2009/04/targeting-the-hispanic-baseball-fan.pdf (accessed 7 May 2014).

88. Ritzer and Stillman, 'Postmodern Ballpark', 103–4.

89. Dewey, *The 10th Man*, xii.

90. The most extreme examples of this are crowd riots where games have had to be abandoned, one of the most famous examples coming after the Chicago White Sox 'Disco Demolition Night' promotion in 1979. See Bill Veeck and Ed Linn, *Veeck – As in Wreck: The Autobiography of Bill Veeck* (Chicago, IL: University of Chicago Press, 2001), 394.

91. Richard Sharpley and Philip Stone, *The Darker Side of Travel: The Theory and Practice of Dark Tourism* (Bristol: Channel View, 2009).

Reclaiming Canada Through Its 'Ancient' Sport: Lacrosse and the Native Sons of Canada in Late 1920s Alberta

Robert Kossuth and David McMurray[1]

Lacrosse has long been considered Canada's national sport and, beginning in the latter half of the nineteenth century, became tied to the nationalist ambitions that sought to promote a national identity through the 'creation' of a uniquely Canadian game. Popular in the decades prior to the turn of the twentieth century, lacrosse in Alberta began to decline after the First World War, becoming a marginal sport played only in the province's larger cities. A brief and unexpected revival of lacrosse occurred in two communities, Edmonton and Lethbridge, in the 1920s championed by a nativist organization, the Native Sons of Canada (NSC). For this group lacrosse represented a natural means to promote their 'Canada First' ideology to young male Albertans. In Edmonton, the Native Sons sponsored a senior men's lacrosse team that garnered some local and regional attention, while attempts by the Lethbridge assembly to promote youth lacrosse in 1927 were largely unsuccessful. Despite the continuing affinity between Canadian nationalism and lacrosse, the NSC were ineffective in their efforts to revive interest in the sport. The 'national' game did not provide nativists in Alberta the platform they sought to promote their nationalist agenda.

Officially acknowledged as Canada's national summer sport on 12 May 1994 with the passing of Bill C-212,[2] lacrosse finally assumed the position of official prominence first proposed for it more than a century earlier. The history of lacrosse in Canada remains closely tied to the nationalist ambitions of men such as Dr W. George Beers who, in the second half of the nineteenth century, sought to promote a Canadian national identity through this sport re-imagined from its First Nations origins. In the decades prior to the turn of the twentieth century lacrosse enjoyed broad-based popularity in Canada including within settlements found in the newly colonized lands that became the Province of Alberta in 1905. By the time of the First World War, lacrosse's popularity in this region declined precipitously, becoming a minor sport played only sporadically in the province's larger communities including Edmonton, Calgary, Medicine Hat, and Lethbridge through the 1920s. As distinguished Canadian sport historian Alan Metcalfe notes, lacrosse never did develop strong roots in Alberta when compared to the west coast, Ontario, and Montreal where the sport thrived.[3] In Alberta, in the years following World War One, a brief and unexpected, if limited, revival of lacrosse occurred in at least two communities, Edmonton and Lethbridge, spurred in part by rising nationalist sentiments.

Attempts to restore lacrosse in Edmonton and Lethbridge preceded and were distinct from the emergence of indoor box lacrosse in the early 1930s. In this instance, the field form of lacrosse reemerged as part of a broader response to growing nationalism prior to

1927, the year of Canada's Diamond Jubilee anniversary of Confederation. The Native Sons of Canada (NSC), a nativist organization, sought to utilize lacrosse as a means to promote a Canadian national identity and represented an element of this broader nationalist movement. A fraternal organization formed in 1921 in British Columbia, the NSC sought to promote the interests of Canadian born (native) residents above groups and individuals who had migrated to the country. The purpose of this organization centred on engaging young male Albertans with their 'Canada First' ideology.[4] Yet, the use of lacrosse by the NSC as a tool to further its nationalist goals operated primarily at the symbolic level, drawing heavily upon the mythology established in the late 1800s that tied the sport to broader attempts to construct a Canadian national identity. For all practical purposes, lacrosse and those who sought to promote it in the 1920s experienced limited success in capturing the interest or support of Albertans.

As a national organization that expanded from Canada's west to east in the 1920s, the NSC appeared in Alberta during a period of social, economic, and political transformation. The Province of Alberta, formed in 1905, represented a tangible example of the nationalist project commenced at Confederation that sought to construct a country that spanned from sea to sea. Opened to settlement at the turn-of-the-twentieth century, migrants from the United States, Germany, Ukraine and Scandinavia comprised early settlers along with those who moved from the eastern provinces.[5] At the conclusion of the First World War a brief recession in Alberta discouraged new settlers, however through the second half of the decade as the economy improved the federal government facilitated the immigration of more than 72,000 central and eastern Europeans to the province.[6] Thus, by the late 1920s, as social and economic forces stoked nationalist sentiments in the province, the NSC emerged as a voice focused on the preservation and advancement of the interests of native Canadians. The NSC's 'Canada First' advocacy included a variety of political, economic, and social initiatives ranging from opposing the employment of non-Canadians in government positions to symbolic actions including the call for local assemblies to support the revival of lacrosse.

The involvement of the NSC in lacrosse and other sports in Alberta and Canada during the 1920s must be contextualized within several areas of historical inquiry. First, the rich and detailed historical examinations of the sport of lacrosse, particularly during the late nineteenth century, provides insight into the sport's ties to the larger project of establishing a Canadian national identity. The broader thesis integral to this study maintains that sport has provided a means to promote a national consciousness. Secondly, situated within the study of Canadian history, are works that address the emergence and impact of Canadian nativism in the early decades of the twentieth century, of which the NSC represents one exemplar. A third, more limited body of literature that informs this study are investigations of sport, specifically lacrosse, in local and regional settings within Alberta. Finally, engaging ideas related to the nostalgic reminiscences to earlier times, specifically the pioneering era of European colonization and settlement of Alberta when lacrosse first became established, provides some understanding of the motivations underlying the actions of men who viewed lacrosse as a vehicle to promote a new vision of Canada. From these seemingly disparate perspectives, examining the actions of NSC members at both the national and local levels, provides a way to assess how lacrosse came to be positioned as a medium to consolidate and provide one answer to the question of what it meant to be Canadian. Although attempts by NSC assemblies in Edmonton and Lethbridge resulted in limited success reviving lacrosse in the 1920s, the broader ideological and political reasons behind the undertaking provide strong evidence of the enduring nexus between sport, in this case lacrosse, and attempts to forge a Canadian national identity.

Lacrosse and Canadian Nationalism: Historical Context

Historical examinations of lacrosse in Canada have largely focused on the sport's early history prior to the First World War. The appropriation and adaptation of Aboriginal physical culture practices including *baggataway* and *tewaarathon* into the sport of lacrosse,[7] and the ensuing adoption and promotion of the sport by influential middle-class men such as Beers, has received comprehensive attention.[8] As a result, this inquiry will not undertake an exhaustive review of how and why lacrosse became an organized sport between the 1850s and the turn of the twentieth century. Relevant to this study are the reasons lacrosse came to be tied to the larger social and political project of promoting Canadian nationalism, and specifically how lacrosse emerged as a symbol for forging a national identity through the moniker of 'Canada's national game'. Specifically, lacrosse emerged as a means to counter the 'foreign' influence of games such as cricket and curling. To understand the construction of this enduring bond between Canadian nationalism and lacrosse, and the reasons why an organization like the NSC would look to the sport to promote their nativist agenda, requires consideration of the foundational period during the late 1800s when lacrosse became a symbol of an emergent Canadian consciousness.

The construction of lacrosse as the archetypal Canadian sport materialized, according to Alan Metcalfe, in Montreal through the efforts of 'young lacrossists … typified by George Beers, the father of lacrosse … [a]n avowed Canadian nationalist [who] consistently promoted lacrosse as Canada's national game'.[9] The attraction of lacrosse for middle-class men such as Beers revolved around its status as a uniquely Canadian practice that also adhered appropriately to British values. As cultural historian Gillian Poulter notes, lacrosse had 'symbolic appeal … [as] an appropriation and secularization of a significant Aboriginal ritual … a means by which British colonists could prove their claim to being Canadian through "taming" and supplanting the original Canadian *ethnie*, or folk'.[10] Evidence suggests that lacrosse emerged as a manufactured symbol representing a specific Anglo-Canadian identity during its halcyon days between 1867 and 1885.[11]

Lacrosse emerged as Canada's national game in the two decades following Confederation, a product of both the sport's early popularity among middle-class participants and the successful linking of symbolic meanings associated with national identity to the sport. The initial phase of this process coincided with the efforts of Beers who successfully positioned lacrosse as 'Cultural performance [that] was a way to claim ownership – of the land, of its Indigenous peoples, and ultimately of a Canadian identity'.[12] Through the assimilation of Aboriginal cultural practices such as lacrosse, colonists could claim to have 'invented' these activities. This cultural appropriation served to both affix the origins of Canada to the period of colonization, while legitimizing nationhood not only through the formation of a nation state, but also by constructing a national history.[13] Lacrosse, in the period immediately following Confederation, represented a highly visible symbol of this nationalist agenda. According to First Nations and Canadian sport scholar Michael Robidoux, 'lacrosse was a display of rugged, brutal, and aggressive behaviours that were said to embody what it meant to be a Canadian settler in this unforgiving northern territory'.[14] This repositioning of lacrosse as Canada's sport served to distance English-speaking colonists from their British roots in a way that both physically and figuratively provided a path to establishing a new national identity.

At the time of Confederation, lacrosse represented a relatively minor sport confined primarily to the region in-and-around Montreal. The sport grew rapidly in the spring of 1867 multiplying from ten clubs to eighty by October of that year.[15] The formation of the National Lacrosse Association (NLA) in September 1867 under the leadership of Beers capitalized on this rapid expansion, although, as Metcalfe explains, by 1871 the enthusiasm for the sport had begun to wane.[16] Between the mid-1870s and mid-1880s a number of divisive issues arose within the sport including violent play and questions concerning the administration of Canadian lacrosse.[17] Despite these complications, the creation of the NLA represented a 'brilliant stroke of promotional strategy … [representing] part of Beers' drive to enshrine lacrosse as Canada's national game'.[18] In his zeal to promote the game Beers pronounced that lacrosse had been sanctified as Canada's national game through an Act of Parliament. Despite this not having been the case, many Canadians remained willing and eager to accept and enable the 'national game' myth.[19] Thus, in the period immediately following Confederation the romantic mythology surrounding lacrosse had permanently implanted itself in the nation's consciousness.

Explanations as to why lacrosse slowly declined in popularity between 1885 and the First World War, despite having become a national sport geographically over this period, focus primarily on the problems created by conflicts between professional and amateur elements of the game.[20] This decline, suggests Gillian Poulter, occurred in large part because of the increasing difficulty 'to hold it up as a "gentlemanly" and "civilized game"'.[21] Whether the cause of lacrosse's difficulties emerged due to class prejudices, or because the player base narrowed as a result of inadequate youth programs,[22] the sport did begin to decline in popularity by the early 1900s. Poulter speculates that the practical concerns of professionalism and violence were anathema to the image of Canada as a respectable and civilized nation. Thus, the decline of lacrosse as a popular sport can be attributed to both tangible issues along with this loss of respectability that 'result[ed in] its diminishing value as a national signifier'.[23] Canadian historian Nancy Bouchier echoes this sentiment, stating that as the sport became more violent and no longer embodied the valued character traits of Muscular Christianity – 'teamwork, self-sacrifice, courage, manliness and achievement'[24] – lacrosse 'did not live up to the expectations as a truly national, respectable game'.[25] Finally, Poulter notes, 'After 1885, a growing divergence of Canadian and British political and commercial interests … the struggle over professionalism and … an inadequate minor [youth] program' all coalesced to detract from the prestige that surrounded lacrosse the previous two decades.[26]

The degree to which an ideological divide existed based on lacrosse's ability to symbolically encapsulate a middle-class Canadian national identity can be disputed, yet it is clear that by 1914 the sport no longer engaged Canadians in the way it had a generation previously. What can be suggested is that lacrosse's initial popularity emerged, at least in part, from the successful positioning of the sport as Canada's national game. Although the link between lacrosse and Canadian nationalism became obscured, the foundational connection remained part of the larger mythology surrounding the birth of the nation. For some elements of Canadian society, specifically men from (or those who aspired to join) the middle class, the symbolic link between lacrosse and Canadian national identity persisted.

By the start of the First World War, lacrosse's popularity had declined precipitously in many regions of the country.[27] When compared to baseball, Canadian football, and ice hockey,[28] lacrosse no longer captured the far-reaching interest of sporting men. For example, in Lethbridge, Alberta, lacrosse nearly disappeared by the First World War.[29] Following the war, few if any meaningful efforts to reestablish the sport in the city emerged. In Alberta lacrosse did not disappear completely, persisting to various degrees in larger population centres including Calgary, Edmonton, and Medicine Hat. In the late summer of 1919, for example, lacrosse groups in Calgary, Edmonton, Lethbridge and Medicine Hat reached an arrangement to determine which city would represent Alberta at the upcoming Canadian amateur lacrosse championships in Winnipeg.[30] The following spring, enthusiasts in Edmonton[31] and Lethbridge[32] considered the prospects for the sport in their cities. In Edmonton, through the early 1920s, the sport's future remained uncertain. A 1922 initiative undertaken by local boy scouts proclaimed that 'The healthy, manly and typically Canadian game of lacrosse is to be revived in the city this summer'.[33] A year later another nationalistic appeal underscored the prospect of reviving lacrosse in Edmonton, in this instance the impetus emerged from the possibility of playing a match against a touring team from England,[34] while the season culminated with a home and away series against Calgary that September.[35] Though lacrosse in Edmonton persisted through the mid-1920s, in Lethbridge the sport completely disappeared by 1923. The purchase of six-dozen lacrosse sticks in 1919 by the Lethbridge Amateur Athletics Association indicated the sportsmen in the city anticipated a bright future for the sport.[36] Yet, by 1922, a failed 'Old Timer's' game against Medicine Hat sealed the sport's fate in the city, where one local scribe pronounced 'the lacrosse match … was far from being a revival of the of the grand old game. It was a death agony'.[37] The inability to attract local youths saw the sport disappear altogether from the city's athletic landscape. In comparison to lacrosse's dearth of youth participation, hockey in Alberta through the 1920s included youth level teams in a variety of leagues that received support from both local enthusiast and the Alberta Hockey Association.[38]

In Alberta following the war, attempts by enthusiasts to reestablish lacrosse resulted in limited success. In addition to the efforts noted above, two examples, Edmonton in the mid 1920s[39] and Lethbridge in 1927,[40] are directly tied to the efforts of local NSC chapters that sought to revive the sport in their community. Given the sporadic presence of lacrosse in these communities during the early 1920s, efforts to restore the sport relied on appeals to broader nationalist sentiments to revive the national game. Efforts to restore the game at this time also took place nationally. For example, in 1925 the Canadian Amateur Lacrosse Association 'inaugurated a campaign to put the Canadian national summer game in the schools of our country. They believe that in lacrosse and hockey, the two national games, we have the best moral, physical and mental developers of any games known to the athletic world'.[41] This narrative of reviving Canada's national game fit seamlessly with the ideological focus of the NSC membership, who clearly aligned their efforts with the historically relevant patriotic and nationalist sentiment employed by Beers to promote lacrosse 60 years earlier.

Nativism and the NSC

Who comprised the NSC and what was its interest in reviving lacrosse in Canada and Alberta by the mid-1920s? The NSC, a fraternal organization founded in Victoria, British Columbia in the fall of 1921, sought to promote a 'Canada First' nativist movement.[42] The NSC's agenda focused on promoting the interests of native-born Canadians and improving the country through policies supporting the interests of native Canadians over those they believed favoured non-Canadians. For nativist organizations like the NSC, being born in Canada represented the critical requirement for being considered a Canadian. Historian Mary Vipond argues that the NSC formed 'with the explicit intention of competing with such other fraternal organizations as the Sons of Scotland, and Sons of Ireland for the loyalty of Canadian-born men'.[43] As nativism existed in early twentieth century Canada, the NSC represented a moderate organization compared to the more radical and racially motivated Klu Klux Klan and National Association of Canada.[44] Alberta historian Howard Palmer notes these more extreme organizations primarily focused on the immigration of non-Anglo Saxons to Canada, generally seeking measures to exclude these peoples without exception. In contrast, the more moderate NSC did not seek to exclude non-Canadians outright, but did engage in initiatives to promote the interests of Canadian-born citizens.

Defining the form of nativism adopted by the NSC involves the consideration of how nationalism and national interests emerged out of the collective actions taken by group members. As American historian Richard Jensen suggests, 'Nativism ... proclaims the superiority of a cultural nation, based on language and customs, and forces outsiders to the periphery, if not expelling them altogether'.[45] According to William H. Katterberg, a cultural historian of the United States and Canada, nativism is a broad term used by 'North American scholars to describe anti-Catholic, anti-immigrant, racist, and antiradical agitation ... and, like nationalism, it originates in common customs, religion, and ethnicity'.[46] The NSC, as a nativist fraternal society, concerned itself with issues related to the place of native Canadians in Canada. This nativist activism included a campaign to formalize 'Canadian' as a distinct racial category through agitating to have this designation added to the national census.[47] Additionally, the NSC sought to reform immigration policy. The NSC's primary immigration concern revolved around British immigrants who it believed had become disproportionally represented in the Canadian civil service at the expense of native-born Canadians.[48] Although the NSC did not advocate for Canada to break away from the British Empire, it did call for the creation and promotion of Canadian symbols to distance Canada from Britain. To these ends, the NSC championed reforms including adopting a Canadian flag, a national anthem, and the appointment of a Canadian-born Governor General.[49] These symbols, for the NSC, represented important markers demonstrating an independent and sovereign Canada, ultimately serving to promote the interests of native-born Canadians.

A number of motivations underlay the formation and growth of the NSC in the 1920s. The conclusion of the First World War prompted many Canadians to consider whether the time was right for Canada to take its rightful place as an autonomous participant on the world stage. The interwar years, according to Katterberg, represented a period during which Anglo Canadians acknowledged their British roots while simultaneously advocating for Canadian nationalism.[50] Preparations for the Diamond Jubilee in 1927 provided the backdrop for a growing movement to assert a distinct national identity. The government of Canada passed legislation in February of that year to 'coordinate Jubilee Celebrations'.[51] Canadian historian Robert Cupido notes that architects of Canadian nationalism at this time believed that memories and traditions held in common represented the key to forging a national consciousness; the Jubilee celebrations represented a timely means to bring focus to the celebration of Confederation and national identity.[52] It is unsurprising that the NSC saw itself at the centre of creating and affirming the growing patriotism associated with Canada's Diamond Jubilee. In the opening paragraph of the NSC's official five-year history, written in 1927, Grand Historian V.L. Denton wrote:

> the tremendous patriotic fervour which has spread across our land from Atlantic to Pacific Shores has in large measure been developed and accentuated by the united efforts of 90 assemblies of the NSC.[53]

The hyperbole of this statement is obvious considering the organization had only recently emerged from its stronghold in British Columbia,[54] yet it provides useful insight into the degree to which the NSC drew its relevancy form the perceived role the organization had assumed in the broader project of establishing a truly Canadian-centred consciousness.

As a relatively moderate nativist organization, the NSC did not demonstrate an excessively intractable stance toward non-Anglo Saxons, particularly if they were native-born Canadians. The NSC embraced all First Nations peoples in Canada who were affectionately referred to as 'the original Canadians'.[55] French Canadian sociologist Sylvie Lacombe, in her analysis of the *Beaver Canada First* publication produced by the NSC between 1928 and 1930, demonstrated that French Canadians received positive representation in many of the publication's articles, reflective of an ongoing and sincere attempt to recognize the important contributions of French Canadians in the construction of the country.[56] In one instance, at the 1926 annual meeting of the NSC, a resolution proposed by the Kamloops, British Columbia Assembly No. 10 sought national support to lobby the government to deport several Japanese teachers who had been allowed to enter the country. In a measured response the national assembly disagreed with the Kamloops chapter stating that the Japanese teachers had complied with all immigration requirements, and more importantly had the right to teach people in Canada who wanted to learn the Japanese language.[57] This example provides a measure of understanding regarding the complex nature of the nativist stance adopted by the NSC. As an umbrella organization, the NSC sought to provide Canadian nationalists with a voice. Although membership remained restricted to men born in Canada,[58] there seemed to have been little appetite to promote their interests at the expense of those who possessed limited social and political power. As the NSC expanded across the country in the latter half of the 1920s it became an increasingly inclusive organization that sought to advance its platform through the formation of local assemblies from coast to coast.

Although the NSC originated in British Columbia, by the late 1920s local assemblies were active in communities from British Columbia to Quebec.[59] (Figure 1) By adopting a nativist approach that sought less to exclude others and more to promote initiatives that would strengthen Canada as a sovereign nation, the NSC held the interests of native-born Canadians as being paramount. Rank-and-file members of NSC were drawn largely from upwardly striving lower-class men along with elements of the middle class. Occupations indicated in the ranks of the membership included clerks, shopkeepers, salesmen, teachers, and small businessmen, many of who were World War One veterans.[60] The national leadership of the NSC, in the 1920s, almost exclusively hailed from British Columbia.

Figure 1.   Native Sons of Canada Float (Lethbridge) c. 1930s (Courtesy of the Galt Museum and Archives)

The organization's leaders were politically active businessmen and professionals who were not aligned with any single political party.[61] Thus, Canadian middle-class interests represented the core values of the NSC, and given the composition of the leadership it is unsurprising that use of sport as a medium to advance the organization's interest arose early on in the society's existence.

At the1924 meeting of the Grand Council, the NSC specifically addressed the role of sport in the organization suggesting that 'Athletic Sports are endorsed but the time was not considered opportune for the establishment of purely Athletic Assemblies'.[62] As Mary Vipond observes, the NSC, as a fraternal organization, provided a variety of benefits to its members including social gatherings, mutual assistance, and affiliated clubs for wives and children. Additionally, many local assemblies organized sports including bowling, baseball, hockey, and basketball leagues.[63] Sport unquestionably represented a relatively minor concern of the NSC given the broader nativist platform that drove its advocacy work. Yet, the NSC did specifically advocate for the use of sport to advance their nationalist goals at the 1925 Grand Council meeting. At this convention, the goal of clearly demarcating national citizenship was logically tethered to the promotion of lacrosse as the national game. Following a lengthy debate, Grand Historian Denton summarized the resulting resolutions noting:

> It was further resolved that the Government of Canada be requested to define the Status of Citizenship in Canada by proscribing the requirements of Nationality. After some discussion it was decided to support by every means the game of lacrosse and that this Society endeavour to make lacrosse pre-eminent among the sports of Canada.[64]

The decision to promote lacrosse received swift consideration when the Cranbook, British Columbia Assembly No. 22 took steps to revive the sport in early 1926.[65] The national resolution and resulting local initiatives suggests the NSC, or at least influential elements of its membership, were well aware of the tradition of nationalism attached to the sport. Moreover these men were similarly conscious that lacrosse had fallen behind in many regions, no longer enjoying the popularity it had with previous generations of Canadians (Figure 2).

Reviving Lacrosse in Edmonton and Lethbridge, Alberta

The NSC Grand Council's decision in 1925 to restore the national game of lacrosse resonated with the membership of Edmonton's Assembly No. 17 who reported in July 1926 that, 'A Native Sons' of Canada Lacrosse team was playing a good hand of our National game'.[66] Although attempts to reestablish a province-wide lacrosse league after World War One took place, a fully functioning provincial competition had not existed in Alberta since 1913 when teams from Calgary, High River, Medicine Hat, Strathcona, Edmonton, and Lethbridge participated.[67] (Figure 3) As in the case of Lethbridge, the sport of lacrosse remained in decline in Alberta prior to the war, and did not reappear in any substantial form following the war. The Edmonton NSC's actions, and a similar undertaking by the society's Lethbridge chapter in 1927, represented two substantial efforts to reconstitute lacrosse in the province. Clearly, the celebration of Canada's Diamond Jubilee, Canadian nationalism, and the larger nativist agenda of the NSC formed the primary motivations behind these actions.

The broader context of the imminent Diamond Jubilee celebrations that cast a nostalgic gaze back to events surrounding Canadian Confederation provided the impetus for the NSC to engage in reviving lacrosse. The 1920s, according to architectural historian Shannon Ricketts, represented a period of growing concern in Canada to protect and

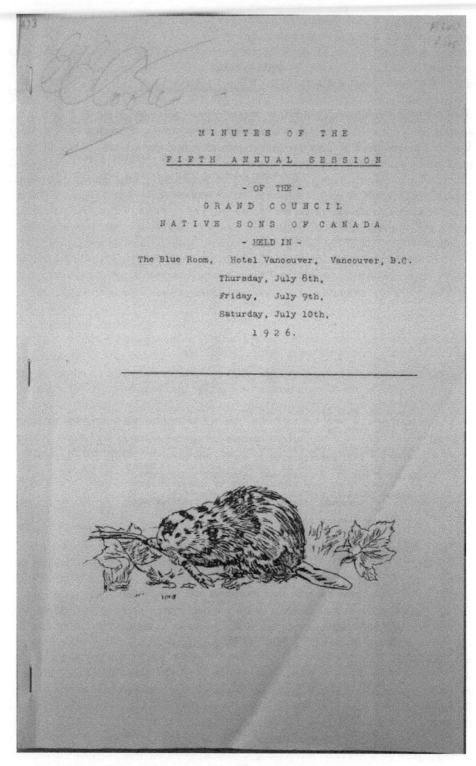

Figure 2.   Minutes (Title Page) for the Grand Council of the NSC, Fifth Annual Session, 8–10 July 1926 [Courtesy of the Glenbow Museum and Archives (GMA)]

Figure 3. Lacrosse Team Posing in Galt Park, Lethbridge, 1909 (Courtesy of the Galt Museum and Archives)

preserve national historic sites and more broadly the nation's heritage.[68] As 1927 approached this nostalgic sentiment appeared in the variety of projects undertaken to celebrate the Diamond Jubilee. As Robert Cupido argues, these celebrations sought 'to foster social and political unity, inculcate notions of civic loyalty and obligation, and stimulate the growth of "national feeling" through the use of public commemorative ritual.'[69] This nationalistic feeling, explored in a more recent example by sport-studies scholars John Nauright and Phil White, suggests that nostalgia in 'Canadian football developed particularly in the latter years of the twentieth century' as fans recalled early Grey Cup contests as Canadian affairs predating the influx of American players.[70] Thus, in the context of sport, the NSC leaders and members recognized the nostalgic lure tied to lacrosse as a game invented by Canadians for Canadians at the time Canada became a nation.

References to the lacrosse's symbolic position as Canada's national game continued to form a common and persistent element of discussions surrounding the revival, or attempted resurrection, of the game in Edmonton and Lethbridge. Lacrosse fit conveniently with the NSC's nativist mantra, allowing an effortless casting of their gaze back to the birth of the game and nation, while fully embracing the nationalist aspirations of the game's first champion George Beers. According to Michael Robidoux, Beers 'called on Canadians to refrain from engaging in the imperial pursuit of cricket and take up lacrosse the new national game, in effect ridding Canada of foreign influences and acquainting the new populations with the soul of the nation'.[71] Certainly, in Alberta during the period of European settlement (pioneering era) prior the First World War,[72] lacrosse took its rightful place as part of a community's celebration of the Dominion, representing one element toward securing the prairie west's place within the Canadian fold. For example, one of the earliest lacrosse

Figure 4.   Champion Lacrosse Team (Lethbridge), Crowsnest League, Winners of Levasseur Cup, 1902 (Courtesy of the Galt Museum and Archives)

games played by the then newly formed Lethbridge Lacrosse Club took place on Dominion Day 1890 against the Calgary Lacrosse Club. A local reporter described the contest as 'a grand struggle for supremacy ... [that] proved a splendid exhibition of the game'.[73] (Figure 4) In 1894, the *Lethbridge News* newspaper republished an article from the American *Harper's Weekly* magazine titled 'Canada's National Game,' in which the author decried the lack of American interest in lacrosse.[74] The article provided a detailed history of game including its First Nations origins, the formation of the Montreal Lacrosse Club, the 1860 match played for the Prince of Wales, along with Beers' publishing of the early rules, and the spread of the sport throughout the country. The author extolled the benefits of the sport for Canadians, opining what 'lacrosse is accomplishing for our boys and young men is apparent to every visitor and nowhere in the world can finer specimens of boyhood and young manhood in their rugged health and strength be seen'.[75] That lacrosse represented the best of Canada and Canadians did not require further explanation for the young middle-class migrants living in Lethbridge, Alberta.[76] Throughout Canada this sentiment would hold true for men who comprised this social rank. This universal understanding that linked the sport of lacrosse symbolically to Canada and Canadians did not disappear even as the sport declined in popularity in the years leading up to World War One.

The mythology surrounding lacrosse and its position as a potent symbol of Canadian nationalism sustained the relevancy of this cultural practice in Albertan communities including Edmonton and Lethbridge. By the early 1920s continued participation in the sport in Alberta persisted in a handful of localities including Edmonton, Calgary, and Medicine Hat.[77] In an examination of pioneer-era British Columbia and the frontier mythology that emerged through the twentieth century, Elizabeth Furniss, drawing on Richard Slotkin's work on cultural myths, suggests that 'through their repeated use, [cultural myths] eventually become condensed and standardized into a core set of narrative structures, symbols, metaphors, and relationships'.[78] In the case of lacrosse, the decision by the NSC to employ the sport to promote their nativist agenda provides an unambiguous illustration of the power inherent within the then existing lacrosse narrative as a means to mobilize this group of 'true' native Canadians to revive this symbol of national identity.

The decision by the national leadership of the NSC to encourage local assemblies to promote lacrosse in 1925 does not seem to have linked directly with the then upcoming sixtieth anniversary of the nation. However, the Diamond Jubilee celebrations certainly presented local chapters with added impetus to promote the sport as a means to highlight their broader efforts toward fostering Canadian nationalism. Robert Cupido argues that the Diamond Jubilee of Confederation represented, for groups and organizations harbouring a nationalist agenda, an opportunity to turn the Dominion Day holiday from simply marking 'the unofficial opening of the summer holiday season' into 'a great national festival devoted to patriotic rituals … founded on a common stock of memories and traditions … a shared history'.[79] Lacrosse in Edmonton and Lethbridge certainly factored into Jubilee celebrations. In Edmonton, three thousand people watched as the NSC lacrosse team defeated a Calgary all-star squad in an exhibition of the 'national game'.[80] For the already well-established Edmonton NSC lacrosse team to play in this game suggests the appropriateness of the association between the sport, the organization, and the national celebrations. Yet, in Lethbridge, where lacrosse no longer existed, a concerted effort by the local NSC assembly to revive lacrosse in the summer of 1927 implied, at least in part, as a conscious response to the nationalist sentiments spurred by the forthcoming Diamond Jubilee celebrations.

The local NSC assembly in Lethbridge, ostensibly acting on the national organization's call to revive lacrosse, initiated a campaign to that effect in May of 1927. The Lethbridge NSC publically announced its intentions by organizing a meeting for all 'who feel that Canada's National Game should be more universally played throughout the Dominion than has been the case of late years'.[81] At this initial meeting the NSC appointed a committee to determine the possibility of reviving the sport. At a second meeting held the following week the new committee sought community assistance with 'devising ways and means for popularizing lacrosse [by] introducing lacrosse in the schools of the city'.[82] Notice of the first official practice on 16 May requested 'Lacrosse players of former days … to dig out their sticks from attics, cellars or wherever they may be'.[83] Over the ensuing weeks the NSC organized additional practices and, despite their late start, remained hopeful for a Lethbridge lacrosse team's involvement in the Dominion Day/Jubilee celebrations. To this end, the NSC explored the possibility of playing a game in Cranbook, British Columbia against that town's NSC sponsored team on 1 July.[84] An absence of any evidence suggesting that the game in Cranbrook took place confirms that, in all likelihood, the NSC failed to organize a team in time. Although including lacrosse as part of the Diamond Jubilee festivities did not take place, the local Lethbridge NSC did utilize the broader public awareness surrounding these celebrations and nationalism generally to champion the revival of the sport in the city.

The NSC's efforts to revive lacrosse did not go unnoticed. A brief article in the *Lethbridge Herald* lauded their efforts,

> The Native Sons of Canada deserve encouragement in the campaign to arouse an interest in lacrosse. It is Canada's native game and flourished at one time, as the most popular game in the land. In late years very little lacrosse has been played in Western Canada, but the Native Sons intend to bring it back into favor.[85]

In addition to the call by the Grand Council of the NSC to promote lacrosse and the impetus provided by the approaching Diamond Jubilee, the election of local lawyer C.F. Jamieson to the post of national Grand President of the NSC in 1926 likely provided a further catalyst for addressing the reestablishment of the sport in Lethbridge.[86] This confluence of factors generated a modicum of interest in the community to try to reestablish lacrosse as the country's 'national' sport. Yet, despite their endeavour to revive interest in the sport locally, the NSC's objective went unrealized and in early 1928 the Lethbridge assembly donated the sticks and other equipment purchased the previous year to the local public schools, thus affording 'a splendid opportunity for the school youngsters to learn this ancient sport'.[87] Through this action the Lethbridge NSC washed its hands of the project in the hopes that school-based lacrosse would succeed where it had not. In this instance, although the symbolic connections between lacrosse and celebrating Canadian nationalism remained readily apparent to the citizens of Lethbridge, any serious interest in supporting and playing the sport failed to resonate beyond the recognition of the largely symbolic position lacrosse held.

In comparison to the unsuccessful attempt to revive lacrosse in Lethbridge, the example of Edmonton over the decade of the 1920s suggests the sport did persist in select Alberta communities, perhaps due in part to the continued participation by youth players.[88] Lacrosse remained a niche activity in Edmonton following the First World War, and by 1924 could boast up to thirty players 'of Canada's national game'[89] practicing in preparation for play against their Calgary rivals. Two years later, several teams remained active in Edmonton including a squad sponsored by the local NSC assembly who defeated the Canadian Nationals (railway) team on 1 July 1926.[90] (Figure 5) By 1928, after a period

Figure 5.   Native Sons Lacrosse Team, City Champions, Edmonton, 1926 (Courtesy of the GMA)

of growth and success, the NSC sponsored team made it all the way to the Western Canada lacrosse finals eventually falling to the Wellingtons of Winnipeg.[91] In 1930 the team demonstrated its continuing strength with their comprehensive 12-2 defeat of Medicine Hat in the Alberta provincial championship.[92] The relative success of the Edmonton NSC lacrosse team provides evidence that in some communities in Alberta, lacrosse did reach a level of stability due, at least in part, to the efforts of the NSC. Yet, both provincially and nationally, this success occurred in a landscape and context in which lacrosse remained a relatively minor sport. The continuing limited relevance of lacrosse in Canada by the late 1920s became somberly evident when Canada's representative lost to the United States at the 1928 Olympic games. A newspaper editorial lamented this loss stating 'Lacrosse is supposed to be Canada's national game … Our national pride should not permit us to allow a land where the game has been adopted to keep the laurels from the country where the game originated'.[93] This journalistic sorrow encapsulates the awkward position of Canadian nationalists who championed lacrosse ideologically, but still recognized that much of the public lacked interest in the 'national' game.

In Alberta, during the early 1930s, lacrosse did undergo a short revival in the form of box lacrosse.[94] As with the NSC's involvement the previous decade, nationalist sentiment and the mythology attached to lacrosse as Canada's national game accompanied the emergence of this arena-based version of lacrosse. For example, in 1936, the *Cardston News* (Cardston, Alberta) queried local sports enthusiasts about organizing a box lacrosse team noting that it 'has been going over big in some centres in Southern Alberta … Lacrosse is Canada's National game'.[95] (Figure 6) According to historian of lacrosse

Figure 6.   Lethbridge City Lacrosse Champions, 1933 (Courtesy of the Galt Museum and Archives)

Donald M. Fisher, box lacrosse in 1930s experienced success less for nationalistic reasons and more for the commercial advantages it provided as an indoor game that could potentially mirror ice hockey's success.[96] Even with a growing interest in box lacrosse, the sport did not achieve long-term stability in Alberta, and by the 1950s the game had largely disappeared from most communities in the province.[97] Similarly, the NSC and its nativist influence did not persist in communities such as Lethbridge. Eventually, the sole vestige of the organization by the middle of the twentieth century took the form of the highly successful Native Sons junior hockey team, an organization with no practical or ideological links to its namesake nativist organization.

For the NSC, lacrosse in the late 1920s did not achieve the stated goal of becoming the 'preeminent' sport in country. Yet, at a symbolic level, the sport's intimate associations with Canadian nationalism remained relevant to the ongoing project of constructing a Canadian identity during the interwar years. The argument forwarded by Gillian Poulter that 'Lacrosse was an effective national identifier but ultimately did not prove to be a suitable vehicle for national unity',[98] might well be correct. However, through the 1920s, at a time when the sport enjoyed only limited participation in much of the country, the evidence does indicate that lacrosse did manage to retain a legitimate place due to the nostalgia that remained for those who gazed back to the sport's halcyon days in Montreal and parts of Ontario immediately following Confederation.

The NSC's lack of success promoting lacrosse widely in the late 1920s in Alberta likely arose, in part, from the disconnect between the middle-class leadership of the NSC and the organization's lower-class membership. In Edmonton, the NSC sponsored a senior men's lacrosse team that garnered some local and regional attention by challenging for the Western Canadian championship in 1928. The efforts of the local Lethbridge NSC to promote youth lacrosse in 1927 resulted in considerably less success. Early enthusiasm to revive the sport in the city as Canada prepared to celebrate its Diamond Jubilee quickly dissipated as equipment purchased to form a local youth lacrosse league went largely unused. Thus, despite the natural affinity between the promotion of Canadian nationalism and the sport of lacrosse, the efforts and influence of these local NSC chapters remained largely ineffective and short-lived in reviving interest in the sport in Alberta. Although lacrosse did experience a minor revival in its box format in the 1930s, during the previous decade the 'national game' could not provide Canadian nativists in Alberta the platform they sought to promote their nationalist agenda.

Notes

1. Email: dave.mcmurray@uleth.ca.
2. Parliament of Canada, Bill C-212, 1994, 'An Act to Recognize Hockey and Lacrosse as the National Sports of Canada', http://www.parl.gc.ca/LegisInfo/BillDetails.aspx?Language=E& Mode=1&billId=4772107 (accessed 9 February 2015).
3. Alan Metcalfe, *Canada Learns to Play: The Emergence on Organized Sport, 1807–1914* (Toronto: McCelland & Stewart, 1987), 208–9.
4. Sylvie Lacombe, 'Fils légitimes de l'imaginaire national: les Canadiens français selon The Beaver-Canada First, organe des Native Sons of Canada, 1928–1929', *Mens: Revue d'histoire intellectuelle et culturelle* 9, no. 2 (2009), 208. The term 'Canada First' is taken from *The Beaver-Canada First* publication produced by the Native Sons of Canada between 1928 and 1930.
5. James G. MacGregor, *A History of Alberta* (Edmonton: Hurtig Publishers, 1972), 164–98.
6. Howard Palmer and Tamara Palmer, *Alberta: A New History* (Edmonton: Hurtig Publishers, 1990), 200–2.
7. Don Morrow and Kevin B. Wamsley, *Sport in Canada: A History*, 2nd ed. (Toronto: Oxford University Press, 2010), 78.

8. See, for example, Alan Metcalfe, 'Sport and Athletics: A Case Study of Lacrosse in Canada, 1840–1889', *Journal of Sport History* 3, no. 1 (1976), 3–8; Metcalfe, *Canada Learns to Play*, 24–5 and 182–96; Don Morrow, 'Lacrosse as the National Game', in Don Morrow and Mary Keyes (eds), *A Concise History of Sport in Canada* (Toronto: Oxford University Press, 1989), 45–68; Victoria Paraschak, 'Reasonable Amusements: Connecting the Strands of Physical Culture in Native Lives', *Sport History Review* 29, no. 1 (1998), 123–4; Morrow and Wamsley, *Sport in Canada*, 78–92.

9. Metcalfe, *Canada Learns to Play*, 24–5.

10. Gillian Poulter, *Becoming Native in a Foreign Land: Sport, Visual Culture, & Identity in Montreal, 1840–85* (Vancouver: UBC Press, 2009), 120–1.

11. Morrow, 'Lacrosse as the National Game', 68.

12. Poulter, *Becoming Native*, 160.

13. Ibid.

14. Michael A. Robidoux, 'Imagining a Canadian Identity Through Sport: A Historical Interpretation of Lacrosse and Hockey', *Journal of American Folklore* 115, no. 456 (2002), 214–15.

15. See note 11 above.

16. Metcalfe, *Canada Learns to Play*, 182–3.

17. Ibid., 183–5. Of the divisive issues that challenged the stability of lacrosse at this time, Metcalfe notes it was the issue of amateurism in the early 1880s that resulted in the disappearance of a strong central governing body to oversee the sport.

18. Morrow, 'Lacrosse as the National Game', 52.

19. Ibid., 52–4.

20. See Morrow, 'Lacrosse as the National Game', 64–8; Metcalfe, *Canada Learns to Play*, 203–18; and Robidoux, 'Imagining a Canadian Identity Through Sport', 217–18.

21. Gillian Poulter, 'Snowshoeing and Lacrosse: Canada's Nineteenth-Century "National Games"', *Culture, Sport, Society* 6, nos 2–3 (2003), 314.

22. Ibid., 315.

23. Ibid.

24. Nancy Bouchier, 'Lacrosse: Middle-Class Sport for Youth', in James William Opp and John C. Walsh (eds), *Home, Work & Play: Situating Canadian Social History, 1840–1980* (Toronto: Oxford University Press, 2006), 245.

25. Ibid., 251.

26. Poulter, 'Snowshoeing and Lacrosse', 314. The declining need for ways to differentiate Canadian from British at this time resulted in lacrosse, as symbol of national identity, assuming diminished importance.

27. Morrow, 'Lacrosse as the National Game', 67–8 and Metcalfe, *Canada Learns to Play*, 205.

28. Karen L. Wall, *Game Plan: A Social History of Sport in Alberta* (Edmonton: University of Alberta Press, 2012), 74–7, 82–5, and 109–12. Wall notes the popularity of these sports in Alberta through the 1920s.

29. The first evidence of lacrosse being played in Lethbridge appears in the *Lethbridge News* newspaper on 26 March 1890. Through the 1890s and 1900s there is consistent mention of the sport in local newspapers. The final mention of lacrosse in Lethbridge prior to World War One is found in a 1 May 1913 *Lethbridge Daily Herald* article tiled 'An Uphill Pull Faces Men Bent on Establishing Lacrosse Here'. This article notes the difficulty faced by lacrosse supporters in Lethbridge 'to awaken the dormant spirit which prevails in lacrosse circles here'.

30. 'Calgary Lacrosse Promoters Discover the Lethbridge, Medicine Hat and Edmonton Demand A Place in the Sun: Talk Now of Arrangement For Elimination Series in the Province', *Lethbridge Herald*, 21 August 1919, 6.

31. 'Lacrosse Men Interested in New Prospects', *Edmonton Bulletin*, 23 April 1920, 6.

32. 'Lacrosse Meeting Friday', *Lethbridge Herald*, 13 May 1920, 6.

33. 'Lacrosse Will Be Revived by City Boy Scouts', *Edmonton Bulletin*, 22 May 1922, 2.

34. 'Lacrosse Supporters Promise Large Crowd at Meeting Tonight', *Edmonton Bulletin*, 30 July 1923, 5.

35. 'Lacrosse Team Goes to Calgary Tonight', *Edmonton Bulletin*, 18 September 1923, 5.

36. 'Lacrosse Promises to Boom', *Lethbridge Herald*, 11, April 1919, 6.

37. 'Old Timer Lacrosse Match See Veterans on Last Legs', *Lethbridge Herald*, 3 August 1922, 6.

38 Wall, *Game Plan*, 115. See also, 'Alberta Hockey Association Will Foster Junior Hockey', *Lethbridge Daily Herald*, 24 October 1925, 6 and 'Wesley Church Midgets Aspire Hockey Honors', *Lethbridge Daily Herald*, 2 March 1925, 6.

39. 'Native Sons Defeat C.N.R.', *Edmonton Bulletin*, 2 July 1926, 12.

40. 'Practice with Gutted Stick', *Lethbridge Herald*, 16 May 1927. This notice was a call by the Lethbridge NSC to 'Lacrosse players of former days … to dig out their sticks from attics and cellars or wherever they may be'. Through this initiative the NSC sought to see 'Canada's national game' once again played in the city.

41. 'Make Effort to Revive Lacrosse', *Lethbridge Herald*, 23 April 1926, 8. The broader national campaign to revive lacrosse included publishing a book 'profusely illustrated with the views of leading Canadian and U.S. teams and … a full treatment of playing rules'.

42. Why the NSC emerged in western Canada rather than the more populous east is not absolutely clear. However, according to Forrest D. Pass, 'The Wondrous Story and Traditions of the Country: The Native Sons of British Columbia and the Role of Myth in the Formation of an Urban Middle Class', *BC Studies*, 151 (Autumn 2006): 6 the predecessors or the NSC, the Natives Sons of British Columbia (organized in 1899), were modeled on the California Native Sons.

43. Mary Vipond, 'Nationalism and Nativism: The Native Sons of Canada in the 1920s', *Canadian Review of Studies in Nationalism*, 9, no. 2 (1982), 84.

44. Howard Palmer, 'Nativism in Alberta 1925–1930', *Historical Papers/Communications Historiques*, 9, no. 1 (1974), 191.

45. Richard Jensen, 'Comparative Nativism: The United States, Canada, Australia, 1880s–1910s', *Canadian Issues/Themes Canadiens*, Spring (2009), 45.

46. William H. Katterberg, 'The Irony of Identity: An Essay on Nativism, Liberal Democracy, and Parochial Identities in Canada and the United States', *American Quarterly*, 47, no. 3 (1995), 495.

47. Vipond, 'Nationalism and Nativism', 84. The NSC argued that native-born Canadians should be provided the option of 'Canadian' in the 'Origins' column of the upcoming Canadian census. See also, Minutes of the Fifth Annual Session of the Grand Council, Native Sons of Canada, 8–10 July 1926, Vancouver, Resolution No. 52, 11, George Gibson Coote Fonds, M260-145, GMA.

48. Vipond, 'Nationalism and Nativism', 90; and Minutes of the Fifth Annual Session, Native Sons of Canada, 8–10 July 1926, Resolution No. 85, 21, George Gibson Coote Fonds, M260-145, GMA.

49. Lacombe, 'Fils légitimes de l'imaginaire national', 213–14.

50. Katterberg, 'The Irony of Identity', 508.

51. Robert Cupido, 'Appropriating the Past: Pageants, Politics, and the Diamond Jubilee of Confederation', *Journal of the Canadian Historical Association* [Revue de la Société historique du Canada], 9, no. 1 (1998), 156.

52. Ibid., 158.

53. V.L. Denton, 'History-of-Native Sons of Canada-1922-1927-', 1927, 1, George Gibson Coote Fonds, M260-145, GMA.

54. Pass, 'The Wonderous Story and Traditions of the Country', 1–38 suggests an often-difficult relationship existed between the Native Sons of British Columbia and the NSC. The NSC was clearly modeled on this senior provincial nativist society, confirming the British Columbia roots of the NSC.

55. Vipond, 'Nationalism and Nativism', 88 and Minutes of the Fifth Annual Session, Native Sons of Canada, 1926, Resolution No. 60, 12, George Gibson Coote Fonds, M260-145, GMA.

56. Lacombe, 'Fils légitimes de l'imaginaire national', 222. It should be noted that at the time this study was completed the 'Beaver Canada First' magazine, housed at Library and Archives Canada, was inaccessible to researchers.

57. Minutes of the Fifth Annual Session, Native Sons of Canada, 1926, Resolution No. 70, 15, George Gibson Coote Fonds, M260-145, GMA.

58. Vipond, 'Nationalism and Nativism', 84.

59. Ibid., 83. By 1924 there were 28 active assemblies in British Columbia and Alberta. The first assembly in Toronto appeared in 1925, and one year late the first Montreal chapter was established. Vipond estimates that by 1929 there were more than 100 assemblies with an

estimated national membership of 120,000, the vast majority of whom resided in Ontario and Quebec.

60. Ibid., 84.
61. Ibid,, 83.
62. Denton, 'History-of-Native Sons of Canada', 7.
63. See note 58 above.
64. Denton, 'History-of-Native Sons of Canada', 8.
65. 'Lacrosse Boom At Cranbrook', *Lethbridge Herald*, 28 April 1926, 6. The Cranbrook NSC assembly donated trophies for a junior league 'as a means of further encouraging the revival of this game, once described as Canada's national sport, but which seems to have lost its hold on the people of late years'.
66. Minutes of the Fifth Annual Session, Native Sons of Canada, 8–10 July 1926, Resolution No. 34, 6, George Gibson Coote Fonds, M260-145, GMA.
67. Wall, *Game Plan*, 61.
68. Shannon Ricketts, 'Cultural Selection and National Identity: Establishing Historic Sites in a National Framework, 1920–1939', *The Public Historian*, 18, no. 3 (1996), 23–41.
69. Cupido, 'Appropriating the Past', 155–6.
70. John Nauright and Phil White, 'Mediated Nostalgia, Community and Nation: The Canadian Football League in Crisis and the Demise of the Ottawa Rough Riders, 1986–1996', *Sport History Review*, 33, no. 2 (2002), 125. The Grey Cup is the historical trophy representing the national champion Canadian football team. With the formation of the professional Canadian Football League in 1958 the league formalized rules to regulate and limit the number of non-Canadian players.
71. Robidoux, 'Imagining a Canadian Identity Through Sport', 215.
72. Generally the pioneering period in Alberta occurred roughly between the 1890s and the 1910s. See, for example, Paul Voisey, *Vulcan: The Making of a Prairie Community* (Toronto: University of Toronto Press, 1998), 6. Voisey points to the decision of the Pioneer Club of Champion, Alberta to limit membership to those who settled the region before 1 January 1913.
73. 'Lacrosse Match', *Lethbridge News*, 2 July 1890, 3.
74. 'Canada's National Game', *Lethbridge News*, 9 May 1894, 1.
75. Ibid.
76. Young middle-class men who made their mark in early Lethbridge, and who were involved in organizing lacrosse in the 1890s included, for example: Charles A. Magrath, the first mayor of Lethbridge (1891), and Patron of the Lethbridge Lacrosse Club in 1894; Harry H. Bentley, Lethbridge's second and fifth mayor (1892–1893 and 1896–1898), and was elected President of the Lethbridge Lacrosse Club in 1893 and 1894; and Dr Frank H. Mewburn, Lethbridge's first medical doctor and surgeon, and was appointed Honourary President of the Lethbridge Lacrosse Club in 1894.
77. A sample survey of Alberta newspapers from the early 1920s suggests that Lacrosse participation remained active primarily in Edmonton, Calgary, and Medicine Hat and the nearby community of Redcliff.
78. Elizabeth Furniss, 'Pioneers, Progress, and the Myth of the Frontier: The Landscape of Public History in Rural British Columbia', *BC Studies*, 115/116, 1997/1998, 9.
79. Cupido, 'Appropriating the Past', 158–9.
80. 'Native Sons Triumph Over Calgary Team', *Edmonton Bulletin*, 4 July 1927, 9.
81. 'Call Lacrosse Meet Tonight', *Lethbridge Herald*, 9 May 1927, 3.
82. 'Call Meeting for Thursday Night to Discuss Lacrosse', *Lethbridge Herald*, 18 May 1927, 3.
83. 'Practice with Gutted Stick', *Lethbridge Herald*, 16 May 1927, 3.
84. 'Lacrosse Practice Tuesday', *Lethbridge Herald*, 27 June 1927, 3.
85. *Lethbridge Herald*, 15 July 1927, 4.
86. Minutes of the Fifth Annual Session, Native Sons of Canada, 1926, Resolution No. 98, 2, George Gibson Coote Fonds, M260-145, GMA and 'Local Barrister Honored By N.S.C.', *Lethbridge Herald*, 31 May 1926, 7.
87. 'Native Sons Back Lacrosse', *Lethbridge Herald*, 11 February 1928, 7.
88. In addition to lacrosse's persistence in Edmonton, evidence exists of high school lacrosse being played in Medicine Hat and the neighbouring community of Redcliffe. 'First Lacrosse Match Here on Saturday', *Redcliff Review*, 22 May 1924, 1.
89. 'Lacrosse Now Popular Sport', *Edmonton Bulletin*, 2 June 1924, 5.

90. 'Native Sons Defeat C.N.R.', *Edmonton Bulletin*, 2 July 1926, 12.

91. 'Native Sons Defeated by Better Team', *Edmonton Bulletin*, 22 September 1928, 21.

92. 'Edmonton Team Becomes Champions Defeating Medicine Hat', *Lethbridge Herald*, 20 August 1930, 2.

93. 'Native Sons of Canada', *Lethbridge Herald*, 7 August 1928, 4.

94. Wall, *Game Plan*, 62. See also, Donald M. Fisher, '"Splendid but Undesirable Isolation": Recasting Canada's National Game as Box Lacrosse, 1931–1932,' *Sport History Review*, 36, no. 2 (2005), 116. Fisher notes that a form of box lacrosse was being played in Australia prior to 1931. Reports of this new game reached the owners of the Montreal Canadians who hoped this indoor form of lacrosse would become a commercial success by attracting fans during the offseason.

95. 'Knocks and Boosts', *Cardston News*, 12 May 1936, 1.

96. Fisher, 'Splendid but Undesirable Isolation', 115–29.

97. Wall, *Game Plan*, 62. Also, for example, the jerseys donated by the Lethbridge NSC in the 1920s reemerged in 1940 and were used by a juvenile hockey team that adopted the Native Sons name. This organization became an ice hockey institution in Lethbridge between 1940 and 1956; see Douglas L. Kempt, 'The History of the Lethbridge Native Sons' (A History of sport in Lethbridge: a collection of papers, by Physical Education 4600 students, University of Lethbridge, 1971).

98. See note 12 above.

The Rise of Modern Sport in *Fin de Siècle* São Paulo: Reading Elite and Bourgeois Sensibilities, the Popular Press, and the Creation of Cultural Capital

Edivaldo Góis Jr ⓘ, Soraya Lódola and Mark Dyreson ⓘ

In the period between 1890 and 1910, British sport flourished in a rapidly modernizing Brazilian city. São Paulo boomed as a coffee export centre for the global market, growing into the second largest metropolis in Brazil. New businesses and industries developed and thousands of immigrants from around the world migrated to the expanding South American city. Along with the flow of new residents came new ideas, new attitudes, and new lifestyles. British sporting customs particularly attracted the attention of São Paulo's wealthy elites and expanding middle classes who saw in these habits the potential to advertize their commitment to modern ideals of civilization and order. The new British-style sporting clubs that sprang up in São Paulo conferred the cultural capital that the leadership castes needed to gain and maintain their hegemony in the city's rapidly changing social landscape. São Paulo's press circulated these new sensibilities and revealed that the city's sporting enthusiasts both reproduced Westernized norms and re-signified athletic sensibilities to fit Brazilian social patterns.

Introduction

In the Southern Hemisphere on the far western shore of the Atlantic during the last decade of the nineteenth century and the first decade of the twentieth century, the uniforms of sporting clubs devoted to cycling, football, rowing, and other 'modern' sports began to appear on the leading citizens of a booming city. São Paulo, Brazil, fuelled by the world's expanding taste for coffee, became a major centre in transatlantic commerce during that era. The city's population exploded, multiplying nearly tenfold over those two decades. The rise of a strong interest in modern sports, particularly an ardour for British pastimes, marked one of clearest signs of the changes imported into São Paulo by its burgeoning connections in the global market system.

Paulistanos (as São Paulo's citizens are known), developed sporting clubs and leagues, built sporting fields and playgrounds, and adopted sporting customs and costumes. One clever entrepreneur targeted local schoolboys enamoured of sport, promising all manner of sporting goods while guaranteeing 'low prices' for his wares.[1] São Paulo's sporting craze illuminated broader patterns of social change in the metropolis as the city's elites and middle classes scrambled to develop new methods of developing the cultural capital that would keep them empowered as the leading *Paulistanos*.

The Rise of 'Modern' São Paulo

During this period, São Paulo became the railroad hub of southern Brazil. By the late 1860s, São Paulo's rail lines linked the Atlantic seaport of Santos to the thriving coffee plantations of the interior, transforming the city into a global agricultural and industrial hub of 30,000 inhabitants. By 1900, São Paulo had grown to nearly a quarter of a million people. Over the next five decades, the city matured into Brazil's economic colossus and largest metropolis with a population of more than two million by the middle of the twentieth century, and more than eleven million by the early twenty-first century. The booming global demand for coffee initially sparked São Paulo's rapid growth but the creation of an extensive rail network also supported financial and industrial development and laid the foundation for its future evolution.[2]

The city's economic dynamism drew a huge influx of immigrants, especially from Italy, Portugal, and other places in Europe but also from North Africa, the Middle East, Asia, and from other regions of Brazil. São Paulo quickly became one of the most ethnically diverse cities in the world. So many immigrants arrived that in 1893 the city had more foreigners (54.6%) than Brazilians in its population. By the mid-1930s, 67% of the *Paulistanos* were foreign-born or first-generation Brazilians. The city became one of South America's largest 'melting pots', boasting a spectrum of cultures from around the world that would shape São Paulo's future trajectory as a global urban colossus.[3]

The city's older elites, the *bandeirantes* who had once dominated São Paulo during the seventeenth and eighteenth centuries when they reigned as colonial conquistadores who ventured into the interior of the region in search of gold and precious stones as well as developing a lucrative trade in enslaving indigenous Brazilian tribes, had dwindled into obscurity. Their descendants, the sugar plantation owners who cultivated vast cane fields by controlling the labour of slaves and *peões* (peons) had also faded from the scene, though the coffee planters who inherited their lands and labourers and in the second half of the nineteenth century slaked the global thirst for caffeine, remained a powerful social class. In rapidly expanding São Paulo, however, new competitors to the heirs of colonial elites emerged to challenge the established powers. *Fin de siècle* São Paulo became a cosmopolitan city in which not only the coffee barons but a variety of groups, including some of the new immigrants, scrambled to establish hegemony in the rapidly modernizing region. In 1889, when Brazil's military deposed the emperor and established a republic that ultimately vested power in the nation's landed oligarchs, São Paulo emerged as the 'second city' to the capital in Rio de Janeiro and a key player in republican politics. São Paulo's elites, the great planter families who arose from the older regime and the new entrepreneurs who arose from the dynamic urban influx, sought to consolidate and protect their power.[4]

The tremendous influx of migrants brought new ways of thinking, new methods, new processes, and new activities that put a new gloss on '*Paulistana*' culture. Immigration impacted every facet of São Paulo's culture, from art and literature to cuisine and recreation to music and politics. In the midst of this diversity, native-born and foreign-born *Paulistanos* competed to develop what the sociological theorist Pierre Bourdieu called 'cultural capital', the power to establish, control, and defend their dominion within São Paulo's social structure. Increasingly, these groups imported a 'habitus', what Bourdieu defined as a pattern of social practices that included both corporeal habits such as sporting endeavours and discursive traditions such as popular narratives that defined norms and behaviours, from beyond their own parochial neighbourhoods.[5] As they increasingly participated in the Atlantic market with Europe and North America which in that era represented the centre of the global system, they accumulated the currencies of 'cultural capital' that identified them as São Paulo's leadership cabal.

During this period, *Paulistanos* began to mint cultural capital that would have served as modern social tender not only in the older imperial capitals of Lisbon, Madrid, Rome, and Paris but in Edinburgh, Toronto, New York City or, especially, in London. The elites and the striving members of the bourgeois who sought to lead the city became fascinated with modern sports, and especially with the 'most enduring exports' of the British Empire, including football, crew, cycling, and English-style horse racing.[6] The elites and their bourgeois allies constructed powerful narratives about the practice and meaning of these sporting habits which they distributed to the masses through São Paulo's burgeoning popular press. Just as in cities in Europe and North America, the mass print media and these new sporting customs worked in concert to enhance the cultural capital that each social practice, or 'field', in Bourdieu's nomenclature, produced.[7]

São Paulo's burgeoning press laid the groundwork for the rapid spread of this new sporting habitus. An expanding readership, which had previously been restricted mainly to the male elite – politicians and academics – began to incorporate the emerging middle classes, including teachers, office workers, bureaucratic staff, and merchants, into a common culture. Immigrants constituted a major component of this new bourgeois. The press soon broadened its appeal, seeking to incorporate women and manual labourers into the legions who read media narratives. The expansion of private educational institutions (founded by religious groups, missionaries, and representatives of foreign colonies) as well as the growth of public education triggered a broad expansion of literacy that allowed more diverse groups to participate in elite and bourgeois habits and lifestyles.[8]

Daily newspapers and almanacs devoted to a wide spectrum of issues included sporting coverage. In addition, specialized magazines also gave greater visibility to the day-to-day habits of 'Paulistana' society, addressing particular subjects such as fashion, theatre, and sports. Publications devoted specifically to sport and physical culture began to appear in the city, including *São Paulo Sportivo* (1892), *A Bicycleta* (1896), *O Sportsman* (1902), *A Vida Sportiva* (1903), *Arte e Sport* (1903), *O Sport* (1905), *Ideal Sport* (1905), *Sportsmen* (1907), and *A Vida Moderna* (1907).[9] Surveying the sporting narratives produced by São Paulo's press between 1890 and 1910 reveals how elite and bourgeois *Paulistanos* reproduced and re-signified British sporting practices and discourses to serve in their quest to garner hegemony in an era of rapid and dynamic change.[10]

These publications frequently promoted British sporting customs as superior to local popular games. *Paulistano* promoters of British pastimes claimed that these imported practices introduced rules that controlled violence, instilled a moral education characterized by a respect for bourgeois norms, and taught values such as justice, obedience, discipline, competition, and co-operation.[11] Though they imported these forms of culture from abroad, the *Paulistanos* adopted them to the unique circumstances they faced as an expanding market hub on the South American edge of the Atlantic world. In São Paulo, these British imports received a *Paulista* gloss.

British sports arrived in Brazil during the middle of the nineteenth century, disembarking with the British entrepreneurs and engineers who came to spearhead railroad construction and other industrial projects that spurred the economic modernization of the nation. South Americans returning from educational sojourns or economic endeavours in Europe and North America also brought modern sporting habits home with them. By the beginning of the twentieth century, these novel imported versions of physical culture took root in South American cities, a trend São Paulo exemplified. Following the British model, British expatriates and South American elites founded clubs devoted to sporting pastimes, from association football and rugby to cycling and rowing to tennis and golf to swimming and athletics to yachting and pugilism.[12] As historians such as Allen Guttmann have chronicled, this global pattern of emulating of British sporting practices by local elites revealed broader patterns of cultural and social conflict. Adopting British sport rather than resisting its seductions signalled the affinity of local elites for modernization as well as revealing their desire to reproduce the aristocratic and bourgeois domination of physical culture that the British elites had mastered.[13]

Interrogating the appropriation of British sport in São Paulo reveals the struggles for cultural capital that took place underneath the adoption and adaptation of these sporting emblems of modernity. Among the Paulista elite and bourgeois, the 'field' of sport, in Bourdieu's meaning of the term, created the conditions for sustained debate on the meaning and nature of modernization. Paulista promoters of a modern sporting 'habitus' went beyond mere replication of Anglo-American and European conceptions of physical culture and re-signified these imports to fit the attitudes and sensibilities of their particular historical moment and location – rapidly urbanizing and developing São Paulo, c. 1890–1910.

Patterns of Habitus in Paulinista Sporting Life

In June 1903, a journalist published an article entitled 'Sport: em prol da cultura physica' ('Sport: in the name of physical culture') in a major São Paulo daily, *O Estado de S. Paulo*, about the benefits of 'modern' systems of physical activity in the open air. 'Enthusiasm for physical exercise currently dominates the spirit of the *Paulista* youth', the journalist proclaimed.

> In every district of our capital there arises, as if by magic, from one day to the next, a new athletic association or, at least, a group of 'foot-ballers', cyclists; wherever there are half a dozen children and an old newspaper crumpled into an improvised ball, a noisy disorderly match soon forms.[14]

The correspondent celebrated that *Paulistanos* had begun to adopt the habits and practices that made the Anglo-American nations the leaders of modern globalization but averred that sport also had deep roots in the Brazilian past. 'Whatever the point of view regarding this appreciable habit of our youth, this veritable renaissance of customs that drove the founders of our civilization and today constitute one of the bases of the Anglo-Saxon superiority, one forcibly reaches the conclusion that no Brazilian can be indifferent', the correspondent argued, cleverly giving credit for this 'veritable renaissance' not only to foreign imports but to the 'founders' of Brazilian 'civilization' as well. 'Suffice to remember that it is a salutary balsam to console us for the great misery of our time. "Mens sana in corpore sano". This principle, so old and true, which, like a good rule, only has exceptions that confirm it, will once again be verified among us', cheered the author of 'Sport: In the Name of Physical Culture'.[15]

Having established that the city was in the midst of a sporting craze, the correspondent insisted that making the principle of a sound mind in a sound body a permanent part of São Paulo's social fabric required active support on the part of the metropolitan and federal governments. 'It is now up to the State to respond to the private initiative, and, by all means, favour this movement of salvation in which many envisage themselves among other peoples', the journalist contended. State support for sport, especially in the schools, would fuel the popular enthusiasm for sport and catapult the city and the nation into corporeal and social modernity. The journalist imagined a scenario in which the state would guarantee São Paulo's hygienic future by constructing the infrastructure,

> the good highways, the various fields and well conserved parks, the clean unblocked rivers, [that] are essential conditions for the development of the taste for games and exercises in the open air, the only ones capable of giving our co-citizens the resistance to the fatigue of stressful modern life, which is, without doubt, the true purpose of rational gymnastics,

concluded *O Estado de S. Paulo*'s scribe.[16]

The publication of 'Sport: em prol da cultura physica', highlighted the São Paulo media's trend of promoting sport as an agent of modernization and a site for generating the kind of cultural capital that in the eyes of its adherents could transform Brazil from a struggling nation that possessed vast natural resources but antiquated social systems into a dynamo that could compete with European and North American powers. It was precisely at the intersection of conceptions of modern dynamism juxtaposed against dissipated antiquity that Paulista discourses about sport fully emerged.

Between Tradition and Modernity: Horse Racing Customs

Debates over tradition versus modernity, over local custom versus innovative universality, came into sharp relief in media representations of the role of horse racing in Brazil. As the historian of Brazilian sport, Victor Melo has observed, turn-of-the-century horse racing provided a fertile ground for examining traditional–modern dialectics. *Fin de siècle* Brazilian horse racing was in the process of a modern transformation as it adopted English terms and standards, developed Anglo-American-style clubs, and imitated the new spectator-centred formats for races that had blossomed in Europe and North America. Conversely, horse racing still bore the marks of rural Brazilian frontier traditions, especially in its gambling practices and its use by certain factions within the social elite to resist modernization.[17]

Media depictions of São Paulo's racing scene sometimes highlighted the efforts to contrast the decadence of the antiquated factions of the *Paulistana* elite against the new apostles of progress. In the illustrated *Paulistana* magazine, *A Vida Moderna*, the schisms became evident:

> After an enormous series of events, reforms upon reforms, it seems to us that we will go ahead little by little, regaining the renown in which we had been held by congenial societies. At the beginning of this year, we had very good meetings, but it was after the holidays, that is, from September onwards, when the gates of the picturesque Prado da Móoca were reopened, that they came under greater competition, and even the programmes began to be made in better conditions, and the races disputed with more impartiality.

There were attempts at abuse on the part of rather unscrupulous persons, who, planning less than honest acts, had, as their sole objective, demoralisation of the Paulista turf, but these plans were frustrated, because some distinguished gentlemen, true adepts of turf, swiftly sought to cut the evil at its roots …

We hope and wish that it will always continue to progress along a growing path so that soon we will be able to be the same as in the past when we glorified Brazilian horsemanship.[18]

In this particular account, published in 1907, the message came through clearly that the social enclaves established at racing clubs could easily retreat back into traditional patterns of corruption if not for the unwavering gaze of a few 'distinguished gentlemen' who formed the backbone of the city's Jockey Club.[19]

Sporting Clubs and Cultural Capital in São Paulo

Sporting clubs that promoted the turf and other forms of physical culture, voluntary associations of like-minded aficionados that had been a key component in the development of modern Anglo-American sporting habits,[20] played a similar role in Brazilian society. A newspaper account of a 1903 party at Club de Regatas Esperia highlighted the role of these institutions in the elite negotiation of the transition to modernity. A story in the newspaper *O Estado de S. Paulo* identified the central role of powerful social groups in promoting the appeal of these new sports:

[T]he success of all the amusements is not only due to the tireless members of Esperia, but also to the chosen and numerous competition of excellent families who kindly accepted the invitation of the society, giving a cheerful tone to the enclosure, not only because of the rigour of their apparel, and for having taken part in the exercises of target shooting, ping-pong and so many other pursuits, magnificently installed in the Esperia.[21]

Sporting clubs provided places where the established dynasties of São Paulo's older society could reinvent themselves in modern settings, lending their established symbolic capital to the newer cultural capital produced by modern sport. They were also sites where the upwardly mobile middle classes could join the elites and share in the new social currency. Certainly sporting clubs were not the only European-inspired locus for the socialization of the elite and bourgeois. The other accoutrement of European and Anglo-American sociable modernity, cafés, theatres, cinemas, restaurants, also proliferated in the city. The sleepy isolation of colonial era São Paulo was rapidly being replaced by the opportunities for modern social intercourse offered by the sporting clubs and other establishments that sold commercial forms of modern culture, as well as in the increasing number of public spaces such as squares, parks, and gardens devoted to physical culture.[22]

The patterns of socialization developing among families of the *Paulista* elite revealed strong connections between sports and arts as forms leisure, as exclusive and distinctive modes of pleasure possessed mainly by the upper echelons of the social order. Sports and arts both generated public spectacles that drew the attention of large segments of the public. The spectacular connection between the two manifestations of culture was exemplified by the creation of a weekly publication that linked them, *Arte e Sport*. Published by Conrado Egisto Pucciarelli, the proprietor of the famous opera house Teatro Lírico, who saw in the sport-loving public a potential crop of consumers for his theatre, the new publication debuted in 1903. The magazine's first editorial, entitled 'Duas Palavras' (two words), proclaimed:

> With the founding of 'Arte e Sport', which, today, has entered the press arena in the certainty that it has come to fill a large gap – we propose two objectives. The first is to offer Paulistano commerce an advertising organ capable of nobly achieving its objective; the second, to provide to all those interested in matters of sport, a well-made weekly that does justice to them with the greatest diffusion possible ... Besides this, the ever more accentuated interests that our society manifests for artistic and sporting entertainment, leads us to believe that we will be well received.[23]

Pucciarelli's *Arte e Sport* spoke to the wealthy elite and the striving bourgeois who sought to magnify class distinctions through both sport and art. The journal manifested little interest in popular working-class trends and focused instead on 'high-brow' art and entertainment, especially music, theatre, and literature. Elitism also shaped its sporting coverage, as it followed the development of patrician interests in horse racing, football, cycling, fencing, and rowing in São Paulo. Like the stories, the advertisements in *Arte e Sport*, pushed 'high-brow' art and expensive sporting goods such as cycling equipment and repair. The magazine also explored the class dynamics that shaped early modern cycling, reporting on competitions between amateurs and professionals and exploring how wagering shaped the sport.[24]

Cycling and Sociability in São Paulo

Arte e Sport was not the only journal that promoted the bicycle as a symbol of modernity. São Paulo's cycling scene generated its own specialized journal, *A Bicycleta*. Modelled on the French publication *Bicyclette*, and published by the local merchant, Otto Huffenbaecher, who imported Peugeot's line bicycles from France, *A Bicycleta* first appeared in 1896 and underscored that not only British but other European habits influenced São Paulo's sporting sensibilities.[25] *A Bicycleta* shared *Arte e Sport*'s affinity for physical and aesthetic cultures, as an 1896 report on a race revealed:

> It was an extraordinarily exciting race the 'Veloce Club' held last Sunday in the Velódromo da Consolação. It was a pity that rain came to spoil the party at the moment the most important races were run. The rivalry, as always, was select among our main high society families viewed in the stands. Throughout the whole time the storm lasted, the fire brigade band, also situated in the stands, played brilliantly.[26]

São Paulo's cycling clubs and velodromes provided spaces for the elite and bourgeois elements of the city to socialize. *Paulistana* magazines commonly featured photographs and illustrations that portrayed crowds that included numerous women, a symbolic shift from the male-dominated realms of traditional Brazilian sport to a more gender inclusive pattern, at least among spectators. As the Brazilian scholar Margareth Rago has demonstrated, although women enjoyed some access to modern sporting practices, they were mainly consigned to roles as adoring spectators. Women provided the ornamentation for sporting spectacles, while men performed the feats and broke the records.[27] Interestingly, cycling did offer a few opportunities for elite and bourgeois women to participate in physical culture. Indeed, *A Bicycleta* systematically encouraged women to take up cycling. A correspondent for the magazine went so far as to publicly criticize Rio de Janeiro's Derby Club for bad manners in heckling female competitors:

> In a Derby-Club race held early last month, the following degrading fact took place, according to what the newspaper, *O Paiz*, narrated: 'In the Derby-Club races, there was a young woman who made her entrance to the race course gallantly mounted on a bicycle, wearing a long dress suitable for female cyclists, a type of jodhpurs fastened below the knee, and these did not detract from her elegance. The fact, however, constituted a novelty among us and the people, full of indiscreet curiosity, began to form large gatherings around the female cyclist, tormenting her with impertinent attention. Up to this point, it was notably irregular that the people didn't understand the lack of reverence they were committing, and from this sad demonstration of their knowledge of the world, finding it perhaps a fantastic thing to have a female cyclist present on a sports field. The thing, however, took on graver proportions. A group of boys began to boo the girl, actually pursuing her, seeking to destroy her bicycle, finally obliging her to seek refuge in the saddling paddock and escape from the race course at top speed on the elegant machine she was mounting. Here there was, besides an attested unqualifiable lack of politeness, an attack on individual freedom, and the police had a duty to intervene and defend the girl so badly humiliated and insulted. But they did not do so, leaving the youths to act without restraint'. No further comment![28]

Clearly, the *Paulista* press enjoyed taking shots at the vulgarity of the capital city's sporting scene. However, *A Bicycleta* ventured beyond mere condemnation of uncouth manners in Rio de Janeiro, encouraging *Paulanista* women to take up the new conveyance:

> We found that two young women of the elite in our society had already ordered two bicycles; some other young women knowing this, decided to learn to ride, and if this is true, we should rejoice, giving our sincerest congratulations to the two gentle initiators.[29]

Echoing contemporary medical discourses that encouraged moderate engagement in physical culture for women, *A Bicycleta* included the inclusion of bourgeois and elite women in its re-inscriptions of modern sport.[30]

The symbolic representation of modernity in cycling represented a key element in the sport's appeal as cultural capital and modernist habitus. The relation between machine and human, between an industrialized product and, in the iconography of scientists of the time, another much more complex machine, the human body, inspired ideas of transcending both human and mechanical limitations. The interaction between the artificial and natural through material and corporeal mechanics created symbolic representations of breaking human boundaries with the aid of sophisticated machines.[31] Cycling offered a cornucopia of biological and mechanical elements that signalled the arrival of modernist sensibilities. The physical challenge, the competition, the technical sportswear, the specialized equipment, the award of prizes, and other elements produced habits through which individuals could identify themselves as members of a status community. Cycling also offered Paulistas an opportunity to test their excellence in performances that were codified on an international scale.[32]

Hygienic Sport Science and Sociability in São Paulo

The modernist ambiance of cycling created a propitious mood for the proliferation of sport among the middle and upper classes. Medical experts lent their prestige to the cycling craze. An article entitled 'A bicicleta sob o ponto de vista medico' (The bicycle from the medical point of view), published in the weekly, *Arte e Sport* in 1903, issued the following alerts for São Paulo's novice cyclists:

(1) Make moderate use of your mount, and avoid excessive effort, such as climbing steep hills, racing at great speed, etc. In each case, this moderation must be established in accordance with the age, temperament, and physical aptitude of the cyclist.
(2) Race keeping your body upright.
(3) Dismount and rest when feeling fatigue or out of breath.
(4) Do not use the bicycle immediately after banquets, that is, with a full stomach.
(5) Clothing must fit the body well such that it causes no obstacle to the cyclist's freedom of movement.
(6) After every race, take a sponge bath and change clothes, especially underwear. Preferably, while in the race, wear light underwear made of wool.
(7) For a long trip, one must eat little, but the meals must be light and nutritious; avoid taking stimulants, as these modify sensitivities and would make the cyclist less aware of tiredness, thereby causing him to unconsciously overload his capacity.
(8) During illness of any nature, never use a bicycle before consulting a doctor, and, if he/she recommends it, there must be prudence regarding the form of exercise the cyclist has to do.[33]

The sentiments that the physician detailed in 'the bicycle from the medical point of view' typified the general medical concern with moderation in physical activities that flourished in turn-of-the-century 'sport medicine' discourse. The metaphors of the 'human motor' and the 'human-machine' dominated scientific literature about the health-producing benefits of modern physical culture.[34] As with other corporal practices, the *fin de siècle* medical establishment recommended balance and moderation in sporting habits. That concept of balance between intellectual work and sporting practice echoed in Paulista newspapers. A 1903 story in *O Estado de S. Paulo* outlined medical understandings of the issue:

> Yet another consideration of value is imposed: one must never allow athletic activity to coincide with intense intellectual work.
>
> The brain and muscles are organs of the same body.
>
> Simultaneous excessive work can only cause general fatigue with serious consequences.
>
> Correction of this functional disequilibrium of the organism due to excessive cerebral work is something that one can only achieve with easy, moderate exercise, in which the quantity of intellectual work is insignificant or almost non-existent.[35]

Calls for moderation dominated medical discourses. An article entitled 'Em prol da Cultura Physica' (In the name of Physical Culture) stressed the need for moderation and regulation, though the author's suggestions for restricting fluid intake would have appalled twenty-first century exercise scientists.[36]

Perhaps the most dramatic warnings about the dangers of excessive and immoderate physical activity came as in the wake of the death of a French athlete who had made a famous wrestling tour through South America, including exhibitions in São Paulo. Raoul Leboucher (Raoul the Butcher) who had impressed the world with his fierce style and his amazing physique, dropped dead in Paris at age 24.[37] In the wake of Leboucher's demise, the newspaper *O Correio Paulistano* dedicated the first column of its front page on 16 February 1907 to warning about excessive indulgence in corporal practices. In 'O atletismo e a saúde' ('Athletics and Health'), Dr Alberto Seabra lectured his fellow *Paulistanos*:

> Many people, even among the cultured, identify athletics with health. The beauty of the façade causes illusions regarding the solidity of a building.

> Our era has been filled with admiration for advertising in favour of physical exercise, physical culture, and all varieties of sports. Treated as scientific gymnastics, physical culture, they arise all over the place, in all tones and in all languages. This movement is pointed out as a resource for human regeneration ... But everything has its measure, and every medal has its flip side ... [E]very physical or mental activity has its saturation point, its natural limit, beyond which the benefits and advantages it produces inevitably degenerate into phenomena of destruction and ruin.[38]

Dr Seabra's reference to the 'beauty of the façade' hiding the flaws of excess not only evoked the transatlantic admiration of the late Leboucher's fantastic physique but highlighted the genteel codes that suffused the elite and middle-class constructions of appropriate engagement in sport and exercise. In re-inscribing modern sport as part of their habitus they associated moderation with civilized propriety and connected excess and over-indulgence to the less refined habits of the masses and the traditionalists. As a professional wrestler and strongman, Leboucher had been a heroic icon of the European and South American masses rather than a paragon of genteel virtues. The framing of his death as vindication of elite and middle-class approaches to sport reveals their tactics in their quest to build cultural capital from sporting customs.

The Emergence of Elitist Football in São Paulo

The issues of moderation versus excess, of refined propriety versus vulgar indulgence, would eventually emerge most forcefully in the widespread passion for the British-invented game of association football that swept through São Paulo and the rest of South America at the beginning of the twentieth century. Eventually, by the 1920s and 1930s, football would become the passionate pastime of the South American masses and arouse elite and bourgeois suspicions about unrestrained behaviours that the game allegedly unleashed among the masses.[39]

In the early twentieth century, however, European expatriates, European immigrants, and Latin American elites established football in Brazil and the rest of South America. In São Paulo, these privileged classes gathered in the exclusive clubs to promote the game.[40] Even in its infancy, football attracted most of the interest of the city's advantaged youth. In 1903, a journalist in the *O Estado de S. Paulo* declared '"football" already does not need assistance; every day, there is a succession of teams, pitches abound, and they're among the best'. The reporter warned fellow *Paulistanos* that '"Foot-ball" ... however, is not enough. Other exercises are of great value, and they do not become popular only on account of the material obstacles'.[41]

In spite of those warnings to diversify São Paulo's sporting habits, football continued to dominate – at least among the city's privileged youth. Football's popularity guaranteed that it would draw attention from the medical hygienists' concerns with moderation. A 1904 article entitled 'Foot-ball: hygiene e conselhos aos jogadores' (Football: hygiene and advice for players) in *O Estado de S.Paulo* warned about excessive practices in the game. 'The violent exercises practised during the winter are readily understood to be more dangerous than during the summer', the reporter observed. 'One of the accusations raised against "foot-ball" is that it constitutes a game that is harmful to health due to the cooling that may occur after a match', the correspondent continued. Ultimately, the correspondent attested that if players followed 'simple precautions' then the game would contribute to the general well-being of the community. 'It is sufficient, after ending a match, to withdraw to a dry place, where all clothing, from head to foot, should be changed', the reporter concluded, endorsing the game as a valuable tool for producing cultural capital.[42]

As the city's elites, immigrant and native-born, took to the British game they redefined the standard codes and practices of the game in order to fit the specific norms and procedures that comprised the cultural and structural realities of the city. Paulistas competed on improvised fields with balls adapted from local materials. The wealthiest among the elite sought to reproduce the British game in a more exacting fashion, importing 'official' equipment and seeking to replicate British terminology, rules, and styles. In 1904, *O Estado de S. Paulo* published a Portuguese translation of a British rulebook, *Foot-Ball Association*, by N.J. Funner and Eugene Fraysse, in the newspaper. The newspaper article detailed specific patterns of decorum for football aficionados. 'During the matches, the players must remain calm, silent and disciplined, allowing the captain to speak and always obeying him', the translation commanded. The translation insisted that 'the game of "foot-ball" will suffer in the public concept, if the captains do not employ all their authority to repress censorable system[s] of playing'. The article warned that '[w]e must not in any way discuss the referee's decision, even though this decision is unfavourable. In such cases, the captain is the only one who has the right to speak'.[43] The adoption and adaptation of the football 'habitus', as Bordieu understood that process, was on its way to fruition by the first decade of the twentieth century among the Paulista elite.[44]

Rowing and the Reproduction of Modern Sporting Sensibilities in São Paulo

If Paulistas both re-inscribed and reproduced the meanings of football, rowing offered a practice where the local elites sought a more faithful adherence to British standards. Rowing became popular in Brazil's leading city, Rio de Janeiro, as early as 1874 when local elites founded Club Guanabarence. Over the next two decades, rowing enthusiasts in Brazil's biggest city built grandstands, established betting offices, and organized regular regattas.[45] São Paulo's residents took to rowing a bit later, in the first decade of the twentieth century, founding numerous crews, including Club Paulistano de Regatas, the first, founded on 14 March 1900,[46] Club de Regatas Paulistano (1903), Club de Regatas S. Paulo (1903), Argonautas (1903), Centro Esportivo Paulistano (1903), and Club de Regatas Tietê (1907).[47] The Rowing Club Paulistano was founded in 1905.[48]

The press covered the growth of São Paulo's rowing enthusiasm extensively. The daily *O Estado de S. Paulo* chronicled developments in a series of articles. A 1902 article reported: 'We know that various young men are trying to found a regatta club in this capital. Hopefully this idea will not remain on the drawing board'.[49] A year later another article noted that '[o]ne more attempt in favour of the development of swimming and rowing has just been made in S. Paulo. This time we hope that the salutary sport will become a fixture in our capital'.[50] An even more optimistic report appeared later in 1903:

> Off to work, rowers of São Paulo! Make yourselves worthy of your patron and do not deny the much spoken of spirit of initiative of the *Paulistas*. With our best greetings, we send to the Club de Regatas S. Paulo our declarations of dedicated support for the development of the salutary exercises of swimming and rowing.[51]

By 1905, newspaper accounts depicted a flourishing rowing establishment in São Paulo. 'The waters of the Tietê River are soon going to become dotted with elegant regatta boats, crewed by fine-looking oarsmen', a reporter cheered. 'At last, the sport of rowing is going to become a reality, which, until now, has dragged on monotonously, lifeless, without enthusiasm', the journalist continued. 'Each club is going to prepare its crews, train them, in order to have them ready, in peak form, to end up on the forthcoming sporting pages', the correspondent concluded.[52]

Paulista crew clubs were featured not only on the sports pages but on the society pages in sections devoted to politics. For the 1903 commemoration of Brazil's Proclamation of the Republic, a major national holiday celebrating the 1889 deposition of the emperor and his replacement by a new constitutional system of government, Club Esperia of São Paulo ventured to the nearby port city of Santos for a commemorative regatta organized by Club Internacional. São Paulo's *Arte e Sport* reported on the cordial socialization that ensued between the two associations from the two cities. 'This race aroused much enthusiasm because it was in honour of the glorious date, 15 November, the Proclamation of the Republic', noted the magazine's correspondent. Club Esperia won the regatta, earning a gold medal for top honours. *Arte e Sport's* account of the race depicted a finish line crowded with the most respectable members of the region's society, including 'very distinguished society ladies' who clogged the finish line. The squires of Club Internacional gave a token of their admiration to their counterparts from Club Esperia, 'a beautiful silver art nouveau inkwell' inscribed with the following dedication: 'Ao Club Esperia Lembrança do Club Internacional de Regatas – Santos'.[53]

As the tales from the competition in Santos reveals, Paulista elites celebrated the social engagements that rowing clubs staged with as much gusto as they heralded the athletic performances of their crews. A 1907 article in the magazine *A Vida Moderna* proclaimed that '[n]autical sport, which has numerous fans, has held splendid meetings, in which frank communicative enthusiasm have always been present'. The journal noted that Esperia threw more parties than any other clubs, including several social affairs during an annual June soiree with crews from Rio de Janeiro and regular celebrations that accompanied races with their rivals from Santos.[54]

São Paulo's rowing clubs provided the city's elite with the clearest boundaries for minting cultural capital without incursions from the masses. As the historian Margareth Rago has chronicled, the crew associations erected rigid amateur rules that kept 'gentlemen' rowers free from entanglements with working-class competitors.[55] In the rowing clubs, the social elites were free to bask in the 'habitus' of their caste without making accommodations for the masses. Horse racing, football, and cycling presented more complex social constellations and more accommodations for mass participation. Still, in all of these locations, the athletic bodies and sporting spaces that emerged from the *Paulistano* embrace of sport clearly revealed the modernizing projects underway in Brazilian cities. In *fin de siècle* São Paulo access to sporting life contributed to the social recognition of a broader bourgeoisie that in concert with the urban aristocracy saw a devotion to physical culture as a strategy for distinction. As the historians Georges Vigarello and Richard Holt have articulated, the devotees of British sport valorized a style that was translated into certain codes, especially a sense of belonging. Joining sports clubs conferred a specific form of capital on members, a currency that was distributed by the rules of socialization and distinction recognized by the social elite.[56]

The cultural capital of sport also attracted entrepreneurs interested in translating it into financial capital. The weekly *Arte e Sport*, for example, was distributed free of charge in theatres, cafés, and confectionery stores. It depended for revenues on advertisers who understood the access that the magazine provided to patrician and bourgeois customers. São Paulo's sporting press advertised products that appealed to wealthy consumers with considerable incomes at their disposable. Advertisements promoted, among other goods and services, musical instruments, dental products, hairdressers, stonemasons, shopping precincts, hotels, perfumeries, imported European goods, shipping companies, factories, stylish European clothing, opulent cafés, confectioneries, sewing machines, printing services, funeral services, and photography studios. The advertisements attest to a network of services and suppliers that had identified a keen interest in sport in their wealthy customers and clients.[57] Some merchants made direct appeals to that sporting interest, the habitus of the city's leadership caste. One entrepreneur aimed directly at the schoolboy sports market, announcing the opening of sporting haberdashery:

> Special store for uniforms with a factory making caps, run by A. BOGGIANI. Specialised in caps for 'foot-ball', cycling – canoeing – driving – riding trams. Badges for associations and clubs, flags and standards, etc. LOW PRICES. R. JOSÉ BONIFÁCIO, 35-C.[58]

Cultural Capital and 'Real' Capital

Purchasing specialized caps for football, cycling, and crew provided *Paulistanos* with tangible symbols of their social rank. Sporting traditions imported from the British Empire invaded modernizing São Paulo at the turn-of-the-twentieth century. These new forms of physical culture provided sites for developing the habits and attitudes emblematic of a leadership class. *Paulistanos* remade these practices into Brazilian customs by creating their own clubs and their own sporting sensibilities that were not merely replicas of British culture but drew their meaning from the conditions of Brazilian life as well. The citizens who patronized British sports clothed themselves with the symbols of modernity and civilization, immersing themselves in this new habitus. By contrast, those who did not possess the cultural capital required to congregate in sporting clubs remained beyond the pale of the new habitus, consigned to the ranks of the archaic and the barbarous and lacking the caps and uniforms that identified the leading classes. São Paulo's press spread these sensibilities throughout the urban social structure while simultaneously profiting by advertising the consumer wares that fuelled the sporting habitus. The factory run by A. Boggani manufactured the symbols of cultural capital while reaping real profits from selling these uniforms to consumers. The elites and the middle classes, who dominated the production of economic capital in the booming region, maintained their social hegemony by also dominating the new 'factories' – the sporting clubs – that manufactured cultural capital. Whether immigrant newcomers or descendants of colonial aristocrats, in the new republic that emerged after 1889 sporting uniforms identified who belonged to São Paulo's ruling elites.

Disclosure statement

No potential conflict of interest was reported by the authors.

Funding

This work was supported by São Paulo Research Foundation [Process n. 2013/15043-7].

Notes

1. 'Ao fornecedor das escolas publicas', *Arte e Sport*, 8 November 1903, 7.
2. Richard M. Morse, *From Community to Metropolis: A Biography of São Paulo, Brazil* (Gainesville: University of Florida Press, 1958); Anne G. Hanley, *Native Capital: Financial Institutions and Economic Development in São Paulo, Brazil, 1850–1920* (Palo Alto, CA: Stanford University Press, 2005); and Cristina Mehrtens, *Urban Space and National Identity in Early Twentieth Century São Paulo, Brazil: Crafting Modernity* (New York: Palgrave Macmillan, 2010).
3. Michael Hall, 'Imigrantes na cidade de São Paulo', in *História da cidade de São Paulo* (São Paulo: Paz e Terra, 2004), 121–52; Boris Fausto, *História Concisa do Brasil* (São Paulo: Edusp, 2002); and Richard Morse, 'Recent Research on Latin American Urbanization: A Selective Survey with Commentary', *Latin American Research Review* 1, no. 1 (1965), 35–74.
4. Mauricio A. Font, *Coffee and Transformation in São Paulo, Brazil* (Lanham, MD: Lexington Books, 2010); Darrell E. Levi, *The Prados of São Paulo, Brazil: An Elite Family and Social Change, 1840–1930* (Athens: University of Georgia Press, 1987); and Barbara Weinstein, *The Color of Modernity: São Paulo and the Making of Race and Nation in Brazil* (Durham, NC: Duke University Press, 2015).
5. Pierre Bourdieu, *Question de sociologie* (Paris: Les Éditions de Minuit, 2011); Pierre Bourdieu, *Coisas ditas* (São Paulo: Braziliense, 1990).
6. Richard Holt, *Sport and the British: A Modern History* (Oxford: Clarendon, 1989); J.A. Mangan, *The Games Ethic and Imperialism: Aspects of the Diffusion of an Ideal* (New York: Viking, 1986).
7. Bourdieu, *Coisas ditas*, 152; Pierre Bourdieu, *Coisas ditas* (São Paulo: Braziliense, 1990), 152; Pierre Bourdieu, 'Comment peut-on être sportif?', *Question de sociologie*, 174–5; Bourdieu, 'Quelques proprieties des champs', *Question de sociologie*, 119–20. The role of the press in the development of 'modern' sport in São Paulo is quite similar to processes chronicled by urban and sport historians in a variety of cities in the United States. Melvin Adelman, *A Sporting Time: New York City and the Rise of Modern Athletics, 1820–1870* (Urbana: University of Illinois Press, 1978); Stephen Hardy, *How Boston Played: Sport, Recreation and Community, 1865–1915* (Boston: Northeastern University Press, 1982); Roy

Rosenzweig, *Eight Hours for What We Will: Workers and Leisure in an Industrial City, 1870–1920* (Cambridge: Cambridge University Press, 1983); Steven A. Riess, *City Games: The Evolution of American Urban Society and the Rise of Sports* (Urbana: University of Illinois Press, 1989); Dale A. Somers, *The Rise of Sports in New Orleans, 1850–1900* (Baton Rouge: Louisiana State University Press, 1972); Cary Goodman, *Choosing Sides: Playground and Street Life on the Lower East Side* (New York: Schocken Books, 1979); and Dominick Cavallo, *Muscles and Morals: Organized Playgrounds and Urban Reform, 1880–1920* (Philadelphia: University of Pennsylvania Press, 1981).

8. Heloísa F. Cruz, *São Paulo em papel e tinta: periodismo e vida urbana 1890–1915* (São Paulo: Arquivo Público do Estado de São Paulo, 2013); Guglielmo Cavallo and Roger Chartier, *História da leitura no mundo ocidental* (São Paulo: Ática, 1998).

9. Three publications were found in Public Archive of São Paulo State.

10. We examined 246 documents for this analysis, including 88 collected from the newspaper, *Correio Paulistano*; 149 from the newspaper *O Estado de S. Paulo*; three from the magazine *A Bicycleta*; four from the weekly *Arte e Sport*; two from the magazine, *A Vida Moderna*; all held in the archive, Arquivo Público de São Paulo. We focused on documents that interpreted the introduction of British sports in São Paulo. The major dailies we analysed, *O Estado de S. Paulo* and *Correio Paulistano*, were large circulation vehicles, and spanned diversified readerships. Both had a specific column devoted to sporting practices. The illustrated fortnightly magazine, *A Vida Moderna*, which was in circulation between 1907 and 1924, exerted a broad influence as an important vehicle of information linked to entertainment in the city. The weekly magazine *A Bicycleta*, modelled on the French magazine *Bicyclette*, showcased cycling and revealed that not only British but other European habits influenced São Paulo's sporting sensibilities. The magazine promoted not only cycling in general but also the products of its owner, local merchant Otto Huffenbaecher, who imported Peugeot's line of bicycles to Brazil. Some of the other magazines also sought to promote the business ventures of publishers such as *Arte e Sport: semanario de rèclame*, owned by Conrado Egisto Pucciarelli, the proprietor of Teatro Lírico. Ana L. Martins, *Revistas em revista: imprensa e práticas em tempo de República, São Paulo, 1890–1922* (São Paulo: Edusp, 2001).

11. Norbert Elias and Eric Dunning, *Quest for Excitement: Sport and Leisure in the Civilizing Process* (Oxford: Basil Blackwell, 1986); Paul Dietschy and Richard Holt, 'História dos esportes na França e na Grã-Bretanha: agendas nacionais e perspectivas europeias', *Recorde* 6, no. 1 (2013), 1–30.

12. Ricardo F. Lucena, *O esporte na cidade* (Campinas: Autores Associados, 2001); Victor A. Melo, *Cidade sportiva: primórdios do esporte no Rio de Janeiro* (Rio de Janeiro: Relume Durama, 2001); and Roberto Trompowsky Jr, 'Desportos', in Instituto Histórico e Geográphico Brasileiro (ed.), *Diccionario Histórico, Geográphico, e Ethnográphicodo Brasil*, vol. 1 (Rio de Janeiro: Impresa Nacional, 1922), 412–14.

13. Allen Guttmann, *Games and Empires: Modern Sports and Cultural Imperialism* (New York: Columbia University Press, 1994). See also, Richard Giulianotti and Roland Robertson, *Globalization and Sport* (Oxford: Blackwell, 2007).

14. 'Sport: em prol da cultura physica', *O Estado de S. Paulo*, 25 June 1903, 2.

15. Ibid.

16. Ibid.

17. Victor A. Melo, 'Das touradas às corridas de cavalo e regatas', in *História do esporte no Brasil* (São Paulo: Edunesp, 2009), 35–70.

18. 'Turf', *A Vida Moderna*, 25 December 1907, 20.

19. Ibid.

20. Inspired by the work of the German social theorist Jürgen Habermas, the sport scholar Stefan Szymanski has argued that the 'associativity' produced by these clubs represents the key element in the 'modernization' of sport. Stefan Szymanski, 'A Theory of the Evolution of Modern Sport', *Journal of Sport History* 35, no. 1 (2008), 1–32. Szymanski's theory has produced considerable debate. Steven A. Riess, 'Associativity and the Evolution of Modern Sport', *Journal of Sport History* 35, no. 1 (2008), 33–8; Arnd Krüger, 'Which Associativity? A German Answer to Szymanski's Theory of the Evolution of Modern Sport', *Journal of Sport History* 35, no. 1 (2008), 39–48; Malcolm MacLean, 'Evolving

Modern Sport', *Journal of Sport History* 35, no. 1 (2008), 49–56; and Stefan Szymanski, 'Response to Comments', *Journal of Sport History* 35, no. 1 (2008), 57–64.

21. 'Club de Regatas Esperia', *O Estado de S. Paulo*, 13 October 1903, 3.
22. Heloísa F. Cruz, *São Paulo em papel e tinta: periodismo e vida urbana 1890–1915* (São Paulo: Arquivo Público do Estado de São Paulo, 2013); Margareth Rago, 'A invenção do cotidiano na metrópole: sociabilidade e lazer em São Paulo, 1900–1950', in *História da cidade de São Paulo* (São Paulo: Paz e Terra, 2004), 387–436.
23. 'Duas Palavras', *Arte e Sport*, 8 November 1903, 1.
24. *Arte e Sport*, 1–3 issues, 1903.
25. Ana L. Martins, *Revistas em revista: imprensa e práticas em tempo de República, São Paulo, 1890–1922* (São Paulo: Edusp, 2001).
26. 'Veloce Club', *A Bicycleta*, 8 November 1896, 69.
27. Margareth Rago, 'A invenção do cotidiano na metrópole: sociabilidade e lazer em São Paulo, 1900–1950', in *História da cidade de São Paulo* (São Paulo: Paz e Terra, 2004), 387–436.
28. 'Sem commentarios', *A Bicycleta*, 8 November 1896, 72.
29. *A Bicycleta*, 12 July 1896, 16.
30. Silvana V. Goellner, Sebastião Votre, and Maria C. Brandão, 'Strong Mothers Make Strong Children: Sports, Eugenics and Nationalism in Brazil at the Beginning of the Twentieth Century', *Sport, Education and Society* 17, no. 4 (2012), 555–70.
31. For perspectives on the history of cycling and the rise of modernism see Christopher S. Thompson, *The Tour de France: A Cultural History* (Berkeley: University of California Press, 2006); Glen Norcliffe, *The Ride to Modernity: The Bicycle in Canada, 1869–1900* (Toronto: University of Toronto Press, 2001); and Hugh Dauncey, *French Cycling: A Social and Cultural History* (Liverpool: Liverpool University Press, 2012).
32. Nicolau Sevcenko, 'Futebol, metrópoles e desatinos', *Revista Usp 22*, no. 1 (1994), 30–7.
33. 'A bicicleta sob o ponto de vista medico', *Arte e Sport*, 21 November 1903, 7.
34. Anson Rabinbach, *The Human Motor: Energy, Fatigue, and the Origins of Modernity* (Los Angeles: University of California Press, 1992).
35. 'Sport: em prol da Cultura Physica', *O Estado de S. Paulo*, 29 July 1903, 2.
36. 'Em prol da Cultura Physica', *O Estado de S. Paulo*, 9 August 1903, 3.
37. Raoul the Butcher webpage, http://www.wwf4ever.de/23585-W4E-w4e-biografien-raoul-le-boucher_news.html (accessed 10 October 2015).
38. 'O atletismo e a saúde', *Correio Paulistano*, 16 February 1907, 1.
39. Interpretations of Brazilian soccer in particular, and South American soccer in general, have attracted attention. Janet Lever, *Soccer Madness* (Chicago: University of Chicago Press, 1983); Tony Mason, *Passion of the People? Football in South America* (New York: Verso, 1995); Roger Alan Kittleson, *The Country of Football: Soccer and the Making of Modern Brazil* (Berkeley: University of California Press, 2014); and David Goldblatt, *Futebol Nation: A Footballing History of Brazil* (London: Penguin Books, 2014).
40. Bernardo Buarque de Holanda, *O Descobrimento do Futebol: modernismo, regionalismo e paixão esportiva em José Lins do Rego* (Rio de Janeiro: Ed. Biblioteca Nacional, 2004).
41. 'Sport: em prol da cultura physica', *O Estado de S. Paulo*, 25 June 1903, 2.
42. 'Foot-ball: hygiene e conselhos aos jogadores', *O Estado de S. Paulo*, 22 May 1904, 2.
43. Ibid.
44. Bourdieu, 'Comment peut-on être sportif?', 173–95.
45. Victor A Melo, 'O mar e o rowing no Rio de Janeiro do século XIX', *Estudos históricos* 23, no. 1 (1999), 41–71.
46. 'Sport', *O Paiz*, 15 March 1900, 2.
47. Henrique F.B. Licht, *O remo através do tempo* (Porto Alegre: Centro de Memória do Esporte, 2013).
48. 'Rowing', *O Estado de S. Paulo*, 20 February 1905, 2.
49. 'Sport: Rowing', *O Estado de S. Paulo*, 30 July 1902, 2.
50. 'Sport: Rowing', *O Estado de S. Paulo*, 31 July 1903, 2.
51. 'Rowing', *O Estado de S. Paulo*, 7 August 1903, 2.
52. 'Rowing', *O Estado de S. Paulo*, 20 February 1905, 2.
53. 'As regatas de Santos', *Arte e Sport*, 21 November 1903, 1–2.
54. 'Rowing', *A Vida Moderna*, December 25, 1907, 19.

55. Margareth Rago, 'A invenção do cotidiano na metrópole: sociabilidade e lazer em São Paulo, 1900–1950', in *História da cidade de São Paulo* (São Paulo: Paz e Terra, 2004), 387–436.
56. Georges Vigarello and Richard Holt, 'O corpo trabalhado: ginastas e esportistas no século XIX', in *A história do corpo* (Petrópolis: Vozes, 2008), 393–478.
57. Newspapers collection, search in Public Archive of São Paulo State.
58. 'Ao fornecedor das escolas públicas', *Arte e Sport*, 8 November 1903, 7.

ORCID

Edivaldo Góis Jr ⓘ http://orcid.org/0000-0002-0521-1937
Mark Dyreson ⓘ http://orcid.org/0000-0002-4792-1072

'Women Can't Skate that Fast and Shoot that Hard!'

The First Women's World Ice Hockey Championship, 1990

Patrick A. Reid and Daniel S. Mason

The rise in interest in women's ice hockey has been very recent compared to the men's version of the game. While men have competed in the Olympics since 1920, women's ice hockey was only introduced in 1998. A watershed moment for the growth of the women's game was the inaugural Women's World Hockey Championship (WWHC), held in Ottawa, Canada, in March of 1990. The event would be instrumental in showcasing the abilities of elite female players, garnering support for the inclusion of women's ice hockey in the Olympic Games, and legitimating women's hockey as an elite sport. However, while the popularity of the sport today remains a legacy of the 1990 WWHC, the event itself started from more modest beginnings. With the Championship, initially facing a lack of public and media interest, the tournament committee made several key changes, including a strategic marketing decision to have Team Canada wear pink jerseys, to elevate the profile of the tournament. Ultimately, media support and approval of the International Ice Hockey Federation and International Olympic Committee would allow the women's hockey to become a mainstay on the world stage.

On 20 February 2014, the Canadian women's team completed a dramatic comeback to defeat the United States in the gold medal game of the women's Olympic ice hockey tournament in Sochi, Russia. The match was the highest rated hockey game (men's or women's) in the US during the Olympics, with 4.9 million viewers watching the game on NBC.[1] At the same time, 1.2 million viewers watched the game online, making it 'the most-streamed event in the history of NBC Sports Digital, excluding Super Bowl XLVI'.[2]

In Canada, 3.6 million viewers watched at least some of the US team's 3–2 win over Canada in the 2013 Women's World Hockey Championship (WWHC), while the total audience for the women's gold medal game during the 2010 Olympic Games in Vancouver was estimated at over 19 million.[3] In commenting on the growth of women's hockey in 2000, Rick Brace, president of Canadian broadcaster, The Sports Network (TSN), claimed that 'Women's hockey has evolved from a niche sport to a jewel in terms of participants, fans, broadcasters and advertisers.'[4]

In addition to its popularity as a spectator sport, women's ice hockey is widely played, especially in North America, with 86,612 registered in programs in Canada,[5] and 67,230 playing in the US. Despite such growth, the rise in interest in the women's game has been very recent compared to the long organizational history of men's hockey. While men have competed in the Olympics since 1920, women's ice hockey was only introduced in 1998. The true growth period in the sport has been since 1989; at that time, Canada had an estimated 4,307 players,[6] while in the US there were 139 women's teams registered, amounting to approximately 2,780 players.[7]

As evidenced by the increase in participation numbers, women's hockey has flourished since the late 1980s. A watershed moment for the growth of the women's game was the inaugural WWHC, held in Ottawa in March of 1990. The event would be instrumental in showcasing the abilities of elite female players and garnering support for the inclusion of women's ice hockey in the Olympic Games. As explained by sociologist, Nancy Theberge, the 1990 tournament 'was an important turning point in women's ice hockey, in large part because it was the first time the sport received extensive publicity, including media coverage,'[8] a sentiment echoed in Elizabeth Etue and Megan Williams' book *On the Edge: Women Making Hockey History.*[9] However, while the popularity of the sport today remains a legacy of the 1990 WWHC, the event itself started from more modest beginnings. While initially not receiving widespread media coverage and support, the event would gain in popularity over the course of the tournament, resulting in what was considered the largest crowd to ever attend a women's hockey game. The planning and hosting of the 1990 WWHC had a tremendous impact on legitimating elite women's hockey.

Previous histories of the event did not have access to internal documents and perspectives from the key organizers of the event. This study benefits from the sources and insights available by its lead author, Patrick Reid, who served as the event's general manager. Reid kept extensive records from the event, including telefaxes, minutes of meetings, financial records, and other correspondence. As part of an agreement to use these sources, they have been turned over to Hockey Canada and made available for public use.[10] These new sources clarify some misconceptions and misinformation regarding the event found in previous literature of the inaugural women's world championship. Importantly, these new insights and sources reveal the critical role played by the International Olympic Committee (IOC) and International Ice Hockey Federation (IIHF) at this time, the reasons behind the confusion over the body checking rule in women's hockey, and further underscore the instrumental role the event had in women's hockey being added to the winter Olympic Games and its contribution to the growth of women's hockey.

Legitimacy and Women's Hockey

Ice hockey is considered Canada's national winter sport.[11] Although men's participation in the sport has been widely studied, the origins of women playing hockey are less clear. Women have been playing ice hockey in Canada since the latter part of the nineteenth century.[12] The first provincial governing body for women's amateur hockey in Canada was the Ladies Ontario Hockey Association (LOHA), formed in 1922 with a constitution based on the Ontario Hockey Association (OHA), which had formed in 1890.[13] The LOHA sought official status from the Canadian Amateur Hockey Association (CAHA – formed in 1914), but the CAHA denied the LOHA recognition, citing the body checking aspect of hockey and a safety concern for females of all ages wanting to play the game.[14] Thus, while the men's version of the game continued to develop at all age and skill levels, the women's game was largely played as a recreational activity, utilizing a simplified set of hockey rules.[15]

Men's hockey teams were sanctioned by the IIHF to compete for a world hockey championship starting in 1920; it would be another 70 years before a similar tournament would be organized for women.[16] One impediment to the development of women's hockey in Canada occurred in Ontario, Canada's most populated province, where legislation through the Ontario Human Rights Code banned mixed-gender athletic competition.[17] This meant that separate teams and leagues for females would have to be developed in order for the game to grow. Fran Rider, president of the Ontario Women's Hockey Association (OWHA – formed in 1975) from 1982–1993,[18] felt there was little demand at the time for girls-only leagues and negligible effort by a male-dominated hockey administration system to create them. 'It is important to understand that support from the minor hockey community did not exist for females, so any progress was in spite of discouragement by male hockey. We had to deal with problems like bad ice, few leagues and no support systems.'[19]

Starting in the early 1970s in the United States, organized women's hockey was overseen by university and college athletic programs.[20] Like many other women's sports in the US at the time, women's hockey benefitted from the advent of *Title IX of the Education Amendments of 1972* (Title IX) that, amongst other equity initiatives, forced the athletic directors of US colleges and universities to provide equal opportunities for both female and male athletes.[21] Despite such efforts female hockey players, like those in other sports, faced considerable resistance in their efforts to grow the game.[22]

In Europe, administrators were faced with the reality that 'women's ice hockey [was] not so popular in Europe that girls are driven to this sport like they are in North America.'[23] The number of registered female players in European countries in 1987–1989 was relatively small. For example, in France there were only 492 players[24]; in West Germany, 450[25]; in Finland, 250[26]; and in Switzerland, 300 players.[27] Some hockey registration reports listed the number of teams as opposed to registered players. Using the formula of 20 players per team, the estimated number of players was also sparse in Czechoslovakia (400),[28] Denmark (240),[29] Great Britain (400),[30] Holland (100),[31] Sweden (800),[32] and Japan (480).[33] Some federations modified the rules for women's hockey, playing fewer minutes per period, while other federations did not allow body checking or slap shots. In many European nations in the early 1980s, local rule modifications in the women's game led to confusion when teams came together to play in tournaments and exhibition games between countries.

Clearly, the women's game struggled to gain acceptance and support from the wider, male-dominated hockey community. The body of research examining legitimacy and legitimation in organizations offers tools for analyzing how these processes work. According to organizational theorist, Mark Suchman, 'legitimacy is a generalized perception or assumption that the actions of an entity are desirable, proper, or appropriate within some constructed system of norms, values, beliefs, and definitions.'[34] In this instance, women's ice hockey could be considered a *subject of legitimation*, reflecting 'the idea that legitimacy is socially constructed and emerges out of the subject's relation to other rules, laws, norms, values, and cognitive frameworks in a larger social system.'[35] .

The larger social system of interest to the case of women's ice hockey is the broader elite hockey delivery system, which includes the International Ice Hockey Federation (IIHF) and International Olympic Committee (IOC). By the mid-1980s, administrators of women's hockey in a number of countries pressured the IIHF to address the issue of creating official, consistent rules for women's hockey. If the IIHF failed to do so, the administrators threatened to form a separate women's international ice hockey federation to deal with such matters.[36] When IOC president, Juan Antonio Samaranch, was made aware of the threat of a separate ice hockey federation, he informed IIHF president, Gunther Sabetzki, that the IOC would not communicate with separate federations in any sport; he had given a similar ultimatum to the men's and women's field hockey federations to either merge or risk being dropped from the summer Olympic program.[37]

At the same time, Samaranch and other IOC members were being lobbied by a number of groups who were unhappy with the inequity in the ratio of women to men competitors in the Olympic Games.[38] One reason for the discrepancy was there was only one large team sport, hockey, and it was only played by men. If a women's hockey event were added, it would require eight teams, reducing the inequity substantially. However, before IOC members would consider adding women's hockey, they needed assurance from the IIHF that women's elite hockey games were played at a competitive level comparable to other winter Olympic sports. Sabetzki realized that for the IIHF to cooperate with the urgings of Samaranch and the IOC, the only possible venue where such an initial championship venture could possibly meet with any success, was Canada. He approached the Canadian federation representatives to see if they would consider accepting the challenge, which they did.[39] As a result, IIHF president Sabetzki announced on 14 April 1989, the official sanctioning of the first WWHC, which was to occur from 5–11 March 1990 hosted by the CAHA in Canada.[40]

The CAHA leadership was aware the championship was a test event for Olympic consideration, and that both Samaranch and Sabetzki were reported to be attending to give their own assessment of the competition.[41] From a legitimacy perspective, 'a central issue for legitimacy research is identifying who has collective authority over legitimation in any given setting.'[42] For women's elite hockey to gain legitimacy, the IIHF and IOC possessed the authority to determine future world championships and possible inclusion as an Olympic event. Thus, there was immediate pressure to ensure the event was well organized and attended, and played at a high level. Although the IOC and the IIHF were now considering women's hockey at the highest international level, this commitment was not formalized by the CAHA until a board meeting, 25–26 November 1989, when the CAHA branch presidents unanimously approved the immediate lobby to have female hockey added to the winter Olympic Games.[43] Two bids (Ottawa and Brantford) were short-listed to host the world championship, but only the Ottawa bid included an arena (Civic Centre at Lansdowne Park) that could accommodate television. As a result, Ottawa was selected as host site 16 October 1989, just five months prior to the commencement of the event.[44]

As the 1989–1990 hockey season got underway, administrators from European women's teams that were going to participate in the world championship complained to the IIHF that the early March tournament dates from 5–11 March 1990 would not allow them sufficient time to complete regular league play and to select national teams. They successfully lobbied the IIHF to change the date of the championship to 19–25 March 1990.[45] The effect of the date change created a dilemma for the Ottawa organizing committee. It meant the world championship would conflict with the Ontario Hockey League (OHL) men's play-offs[46]; the Ottawa-based OHL team, the 67s, would have play-off games scheduled in the Civic Centre, the site of the women's championship,[47] and the 67s had priority in terms of use for hockey games and practices as this was the club's home arena. Since the exact dates of the 67s home play-off games in mid-March would not be finalized by OHL league officials until early March, game dates and times of the women's championship could not be set until that occurred.[48] The result was that tickets for the women's tournament could not be printed and put on sale until a short few weeks prior to the start of the tournament.[49]

Establishing Rules of Play

Since women's hockey did not fully follow the IIHF rule book, an issue that had to be dealt with was establishing playing rules that the various teams and federations could agree upon. In the women's national championship in West Germany in the mid-1980s, for example, teams only played two, 10-minute periods, rather than following IIHF rule of three, 20- minute periods.[50] In Canada at the same time, the CAHA rule for the women's national championship was three, 12-minute, stop time periods for all preliminary, quarter and semi-final games; and for the consolation and championship games, teams played three, 15-minute, stop time periods.[51]

For the inaugural European women's hockey championship, held in 1989, tournament officials applied the IIHF rule book for the most part: teams played three, 20-minute stop time periods; touch icing was instituted; players were allowed to clear the zone on delayed off-sides; body checking was allowed; and, after some lengthy discussions prior to the championship, the IIHF agreed to allow slap shots. Players were allowed to wear visors, but only a few chose to do so.[52] A year later when the IIHF established the first women's world championship, clarifying standard hockey rules and regulations again became an issue.

The IIHF membership declared the following conditions for the women's championship at their fall meeting in Zurich in 1989: each roster would consist of 20 players including two goalies, with a maximum team complement with coaches and staff of 25 persons; IIHF Council member Walter Bush (US) would be the IIHF chair for the championship; players would be required to wear a full face shield, a chest protector and a groin ('jill') protector; players' hair could not stick out of their helmets more than four inches; slap shots would be allowed; neither doping control testing nor femininity testing would be required, but both were recommended for future events; and the minimum age of players would be 16 years (teams could bring younger players with consent of their federation).[53] The Norwegian team would later take advantage of the latter rule and included a 14- and two 15-year-old players on their world championship team roster.[54]

One additional issue discussed at the meeting was whether or not to allow body checking in the tournament. It was the opinion of the IIHF membership that the event would depart too far from the game should something as significant as body checking be removed from the sport. The body checking rule had been in effect during the European women's championship.[55] The absence of body checking was one of the reasons the German Ice Hockey Federation did not allow an invited club team from its jurisdiction to compete in the 1987 women's tournament in Toronto, claiming that by disallowing body checking, the OWHA was staging an event that was 'a step in the wrong direction for women's hockey.'[56]

Hockey is a collision sport, meaning that the speed of the game results in physical contact between players. However, while contact may be inevitable, where body checking is allowed players may deliberately 'close space' between themselves and opponents in order to dislodge them from the puck. Where body contact is not allowed, players may still physically make contact with one another as long as this is incidental to a player working to try to retrieve the puck from an opponent. In discussing body contact/checking in women's hockey, Etue and Williams claimed that 'Although body checking has been banned in IIHF events, body contact is still very much a part of the games. This has caused confusion among players, coaches and referees since the point at which body contact becomes body checking has never been precisely defined.'[57] However, CAHA rules on body contact were clearly explained to all CAHA branches as early as 1989, in preparation for the 1990 event.[58] IIHF membership was aware of the concern expressed by members of the CAHA executive committee – president Murray Costello and vice presidents Pat Reid (high performance) and Bob Nicholson (domestic) – that a serious injury could occur at this first world championship if body checking was allowed, because of the wide range in age and playing ability of the players. If such an injury did occur, it was feared it would set back women's hockey at a time when it was attempting to gain acceptance on the world stage.[59]

Officials of the IIHF and the CAHA agreed on a compromise. The IIHF technical director stated publicly that body checking would be permissible but he privately informed the team coaches and instructed the referees to call any body contact very closely – as if the no body checking rule were in effect.[60] This compromise later led to considerable confusion at the event, for the players, the fans and even the television play-by-play announcers, who repeatedly questioned the inconsistency of the referees calling penalties for body checking during game broadcasts.[61] This compromise also clarifies some misconceptions regarding the rules used during the tournament. As explained by Etue and Williams: 'Despite the Canadian ban, at the first world championship in 1990 the IIHF insisted on body checking, pandering to the prevailing notion that real hockey must include tough physical play.'[62] In reality, the decision was driven by a need to both protect players and ensure support from the different governing bodies, and although publically acknowledging that body checking was allowed, in practice games were called as though body checking was forbidden.

During the meeting in Zurich, the IIHF membership also decided the women would play three, 20-minute, stop time periods, and there would be two pools of four teams in the event, with pool 'A' consisting of Canada, Sweden, West Germany, and a team representing Asia, and a pool 'B' consisting of the USA, Norway, Finland, and Switzerland.[63] The women's team from the Chinese Ice Hockey Association had won the Asian championship and the right to represent Asia in the world championship, but Chinese Hockey Federation officials declined the offer, which was then accepted by the next eligible Asian federation, from Japan.[64]

Initially, the IIHF had assigned 15 officials for the women's championship, 13 were men and only two were women; with the men assigned to fill all five referee positions[65]; CAHA president Costello was able to renegotiate the assignments with the IIHF and replaced three of the assigned male linesmen and one referee, with women.[66]

Tournament Management and Financing

The event did not seem to be a priority for the CAHA, which was slow in organizing the women's world championship. The tournament was awarded to the CAHA in April 1989 and it took until October (five months later) to award the event to the Ottawa District Hockey Association (ODHA) who, by that time, was already focused on the annual delivery of winter hockey programs. The CAHA did not budget specifically for the world championship; it was assumed the event would pay for itself. The tournament was initially organized by CAHA board member and chair of female hockey, Frank Libera, and a volunteer organizing committee. However, without a general manager overseeing the event, the volunteer organizers started missing deadlines. Toward the end of October 1989, the CAHA management committee attempted to hire the event general manager who had recently organized the world junior field hockey championship in Canada.[67] Her salary demand was deemed unreasonable by the CAHA president, so only five months before the championship was to start, the CAHA president assigned the event manager duties to the CAHA vice president of high performance, Pat Reid.[68] Reid was reticent to accept as he was already the director of operations (DO)/general manager of the women's team, and also DO/general manager for the men's world junior team which meant he would be in Helsinki, Finland, for the world junior championship for nearly a month in December 1989 and January 1990 and unavailable to manage the various event organizing subcommittees in Ottawa while away.[69]

Funding sources that were expected to provide the revenue for the event did not materialize as expected. When the IIHF awarded the championship to the CAHA in April 1989, the IIHF president promised a $150,000 financial contribution to the CAHA to assist in hosting the event.[70] A few weeks later, the IIHF announced that as a condition of the funding the CAHA had to arrange television broadcasting of four of the women's games including simultaneous delivery to Europe by satellite, free of charge.[71] The CAHA management committee had little choice but to agree, and immediately contacted both the Canadian Broadcasting Corporation (CBC) and Canadian Television Network (CTV), but both broadcasters had existing commitments on those dates. The only partner available to assist with airing the four games for the CAHA was The Sports Network (TSN), a specialty cable channel.[72] The final contract offered by Rick Brace, vice president programming, TSN, was that the company would charge the CAHA $17,000 for each game broadcast, but in return the CAHA would receive a number of the 30 second television advertising spots, valued at approximately $60,000, which they could sell to sponsors, to recoup their initial cash outlay.[73] Despite this arrangement, no sponsors stepped forward and the inventory went unsold, as did the rink board advertising opportunities which were initially expected to generate $50,000 of income.[74] The TSN 30 second commercial spots were returned to TSN.[75]

The CAHA executive committee members were aware that at the 1987 OWHA tournament, organizers were unable to sell their proposed $20,000 and $10,000 event sponsor packages.[76] Even though the Ottawa event was the first women's world championship and had national and international broadcasts confirmed, the same fate befell the organizing committee.[77] The championship would be broadcast without a title or a presenting sponsor. At the time of the women's world championship, the CAHA was in a partnership with the original Hockey Canada through the formation of the Canadian International Hockey Committee (CIHC).[78] Hockey Canada was the organization that managed professional and international hockey in Canada. The partnership allowed the two bodies to share in the organization of Canada's international hockey participation. The CAHA president approached the members of the CIHC to gauge their interest in sharing in the organization and sponsorship of the women's tournament, but they declined.[79] This decision meant the main sponsors of the existing men's international hockey events would not be contributing to the women's event, except for one sponsor that offered to donate beer for the closing reception.[80]

The Canadian government had a sport hosting policy at the time that provided funds for international events hosted in Canada, and the CAHA was granted $50,000 to be used for the women's world championship.[81] However, the tournament took place just after the Dubin Inquiry into the Ben Johnson doping scandal that exploded during the 1988 Seoul Olympics. The Johnson case proved to be an enormous embarrassment to the federal government and Sport Canada. Consequently, the funding included the caveat that event organizers had to conduct drug testing at the event.[82] The IIHF technical director had already informed members of the participating hockey federations that drug testing would not be undertaken; he had to reverse that decision and inform teams that drug testing would occur.[83] Testing would be at CAHA's expense, which consumed much of the funding.[84]

The IIHF traditionally secured a sponsor for awards for the IIHF Fair Play Cup (awarded to the least penalized tournament team at each IIHF world championship), and also provided awards for the individual players selected to the tournament all-star team. On 14 March 1990, one week before the start of the championship, Jan-Ake Edvinsson, the IIHF general secretary, sent a telefax to the CAHA stating the IIHF was unable to secure a sponsor for the awards for either the Fair Play Cup or for the all-star team, and asked the CAHA to absorb the cost of the awards.[85] With all of the financial uncertainty, just before the start of the championship, the CAHA forecast projected an event loss of $90,000.[86]

With ticket sales stalled, sponsorship not materializing and time running out, the CAHA management committee was concerned the Ottawa championship might occur with little impact, and what the prospects would be for the women's game becoming an Olympic event. To gain some exposure for the tournament, the event manager, Pat Reid, contacted hockey celebrity Don Cherry to request his assistance in promoting the event during his 'Coach's Corner' television vignette.[87] A brief promotion aired the final Saturday night prior to the medal round.[88] Reid also contacted hockey celebrity Wayne Gretky through his agent Mike Barnett[89] to ask permission to have the organizing committee include a photo of his one year old daughter, Paulina, on a promotional poster titled 'The Future Belongs to Women's Hockey', but the request was turned down.[90]

Uncertainty During the Lead up to the Championship

The local sports media showed little interest in covering the upcoming tournament. Unfortunately for the event organizers, the Ottawa media had just experienced another women's first 'world' championship, staged by Ringette Canada, in the Ottawa suburb of Gloucester, six weeks before the women's hockey event. The ringette 'world' championship involved eight teams – six from Canada, and one each from the US and Finland. Canada placed first, second, third, fourth, fifth and sixth, with Finland placing seventh, while the US, who did not score a goal in the tournament, placed eighth.[91] In this context, CAHA executive committee members were concerned that the announcement that the women's hockey championship would be the first ever would not have the appeal to attract media interest or the attention of the general public and the women's championship might suffer the same fate as the OWHA tournament three years earlier, attracting little interest from the public outside of the local women's hockey community. There was only one player on Team Canada from the Ottawa area, Kim Ratushny, and she was relatively unknown in Ottawa as an elite hockey player as she played her hockey at Cornell University where she was on a hockey scholarship. Discussion of the event in media coverage revealed that there were no well-known players, so the event general manager staged an exhibition hockey game a week before the women's championship, to 'introduce' the members of Team Canada to the Ottawa sports media.[92] As an added attraction to spectators, the press release highlighted the fact that the media team would be bolstered by five retired NHL players.[93] The two teams played at one of the main arenas in the city, the Nepean Sportsplex, for one period and then Team Canada played an all-star senior women's team for the latter two periods. Despite the direct exposure with members of the sports media, the celebrity game received no media coverage the following day.

Not surprisingly, when journalists did interview Team Canada players, they repeatedly framed their questions in terms of the men's game. Team Canada player, Judy Diduck, was asked to compare the level of women's play expected at the championship to men's hockey. She responded that it was comparable to a boy's triple-A midget team.[94] Team USA head coach, Don MacLeod, when asked the same question, replied it was comparable to a US boy's high school team.[95] While these comments were meant to be complementary, they only reinforced the fact that the women's game was largely understood within the male-dominated context of elite hockey. This would serve no useful purpose as the tournament sought to establish women's hockey as a unique, legitimate form of competition at the international (and potentially Olympic) level. At the same time, these comparisons did little to boost the excitement and promotion of the pending world championship and the CAHA management committee expressed concerns given the need to showcase games to the IOC.[96]

As uncertainty around the event continued, the OHL men's play-off schedule and the Ottawa 67s games and practice schedule were finally confirmed. There were few quality ice times available in the Civic Centre arena for the women's games and practices. This meant that many more of the round robin games had to be scheduled at midday, at the start of the week, and in arenas in nearby communities.[97] The CAHA executive committee had witnessed the calibre of play of Team Canada at the selection camp. They were convinced that if members of the public saw Team Canada play they would likely return to watch games in the medal round. To address this issue, the event general manager arranged for the distribution of 45,000 complimentary tickets to the public for admission to these preliminary games, hoping for significant attendance while expressing less concern about lost revenue.[98] As explained by the event general manager 'Women's hockey is an unknown quantity, we have to get people out to the first game. If we can get them in the building, they'll be back'.[99]

When the IIHF tournament schedule was first released, Canada was scheduled to play Japan in the opening game, a contest slated to be featured coverage in the television contract for the event. At the IIHF meeting in Zurich where the tournament schedule was first announced, the Japanese IIHF member, Mr Kenichi-Chizuka, explained that the Japanese team would not be very strong.[100] The management committee did not want the first televised game in the championship to be a rout, so the CAHA president requested the schedule be rearranged to have Canada compete against Sweden in the opening game, and play Japan later in the week.[101] The members of the other competing hockey federations agreed to the change.

A Finnish hockey equipment company, Tackla, had a contract with the IIHF to provide the hockey jerseys and socks for each of the women's teams in the championship. The event general manager approached the president of Tackla, Mauri Nylund, to ask if the company would be interested in separately sponsoring the Canadian women's national team, which was considered a gold medal favorite. They agreed on a contract that included a number of items, including Tackla hockey gloves, hockey sticks, equipment bags and gym bags, as well as 150 jackets and 150 sweat shirts for organizing committee members.[102] The few Team Canada players who wanted to use their own hockey sticks and gloves had to either tape over or paint over the existing logos on them, to comply with Tackla's exclusive contract.[103]

Desperate Measures?

Frustrated by the comparisons to the men's game, sparse media coverage, lack of ticket sales, and concern that the tournament would be 'a huge flop',[104] Reid proposed to the CAHA president that instead of wearing the traditional men's uniform colors of red and white, that the women step on the ice wearing their own unique pink and white uniforms.[105] In Reid's estimation, the pink and white jerseys would not only create a unique identity for the women's team but at the same time would surely draw attention from the hockey media and get them writing about the event, ultimately providing the much needed team and tournament promotion the organizing committee to that point had been unable to generate.[106] Reid also provided some preliminary design drawings.[107] Initially speechless, the president's response was, 'Absolutely not.'[108] 'If we go with pink ... we'll get crucified'.[109] It took three lengthy meetings before there was agreement to allow the team to wear the distinctive pink and white jerseys and socks.[110] The CAHA president had added the condition that he would only consent to the proposal if the team and coaches were also in agreement.[111] The head coach of Team Canada, Dave McMaster, and assistant coach, Lucie Valois, were well aware of the lack of media interest in Team Canada and in the tournament in general. When approached with the pink jersey strategy, McMaster agreed there did not seem to be a better option, but worried the general manager was taking quite a risk.[112] Valois understood the need to give exposure to the event, discussed it with the players, and later reported 'All the players on the team love the uniforms, we have no complaints at all'.[113]

To launch the new Team Canada pink and white jerseys, the CAHA staged a press conference on Parliament Hill that was to include the presentation of one of the first jerseys, to Mila Mulroney, wife of the prime minister at the time, Brian Mulroney.[114] Although a team jersey was created with a Mulroney name plate on the back, she was unavailable for the press conference, so Team Canada player Judy Diduck, modeled the team's jersey.[115] Toronto *Globe and Mail* journalist, Roy MacGregor, reported that when the pink jerseys were unveiled, 'hockey traditionalists were outraged. The issue was even raised in Parliament. But the media ate it up, both pro and con.'[116] The two major newspapers in Ottawa published uncomplimentary articles following the press conference. *Ottawa Sun* sports editor, Jane O'Hara wrote: 'Sorry Girls, Pink Stinks. Real Women Don't Wear Pink'.[117] Senior sports columnist Earl McCrae of the *Ottawa Citizen* wrote:

> As if the world isn't already going nuts enough, fast enough, we now take you to the latest example of certifiable lunacy loose upon the planet: Is Canada's pink and white national women's hockey team, in town for the world championship, a dazzling statement of cool high fashion for the future or an example of degrading female stereotype of the past?[118]

While the media railed about the pink jerseys, the Team Canada players quickly defended them. Thirty-three-year-old Sue Scherer, captain of Team Canada said:

> How can anyone say wearing pink means we're demeaning women? Or women's hockey? These kind of bright, flashy colors are the trend today in sports. Take a look at skiing. Tennis. Surely that kind of perception-labelling because of a color is outdated. I'm sorry I have no time for it.[119]

Recounting the reaction of the press years later, former CAHA president, Murray Costello, recalled, 'all of a sudden people knew there was a women's event. I think it played in every newspaper across the country ... the women's game was on the map'.[120] The last attempt at generating some promotion for the tournament with the public was an exhibition game between Team Canada and Team Sweden played in the village of Russell on the outskirts of Ottawa, on 17 March 1990, two days before the start of the championship; once again, local newspapers did not carry any stories that mentioned the game.

From the time of the press announcement to the end of the women's tournament, members of the Ottawa media appeared to become more receptive to Team Canada and their pink uniforms. Reporters and radio and television talk show hosts were describing Team Canada as possessing 'pink power', spectator interest and attendance continued to build throughout the week of the tournament.[121] One Canadian press wire story reported that 'the unofficial motto of the Canadian women's hockey team is "powerful in pink" and no one is arguing with the boast yet.'[122] Team Canada players were aware that the pink and white jerseys and the distribution of 45,000 complimentary tickets were in large part marketing and promotion tactics intended to attract spectators to the arenas to be exposed to their play. Part way through the championship Team Canada's top scorer, Angela James, summed up the pink jersey situation. 'The pink jerseys were a bit of a gimmick. The girls said if that's what it's going to take to get the fans out, fine. We'll show them on the ice.'[123] As one journalist who interviewed the players, reported, 'The players, weary of having their game compared to the men's, immediately liked the distinctive look of the pink uniforms.'[124]

By now Walter Bush, the IIHF council member assigned as chair of the championship, had seen the teams practice and was confident the tournament would be a success as an Olympic test event; when interviewed the day before the opening game. 'I predict there's a better than average chance it'll be in the 1994 Olympics in Norway, but to be in it, you first have to have a world tournament like this', Bush contended.[125]

The Championship

To the disappointment of the CAHA management committee, the CAHA received a telefax from the IIHF prior to the start of the tournament, stating that Sabetzki and Samaranch would not be attending the event after all.[126] Despite this setback, at 7:30 pm, 19 March 1990, IIHF representative Walter Bush (US), pronounced 'On behalf of the International Ice Hockey Federation, I declare the games of the 1990 WWHC officially open.' The national anthem was sung by future recording star, Alanis Morissette.[127]

The tournament had actually commenced that afternoon at 1 pm, with three games played in outlying arenas.[128] According to the game sheets, the first goal scored in this first world championship was by Elvira Saager of West Germany, assisted by Monika Spring,[129] in a 4–1 victory over Japan.[130] This game was played in front of approximately 150 spectators, including a lone journalist, John MacKinnon of the *Ottawa Citizen*.[131] The referee was Canadian Deb Maybury, the first woman to referee an IIHF world championship game. The evening game featured Canada versus Sweden, won by Canada 15–1. The game was played in front of a crowd of 3,578 spectators, including about 1,000 spectators using complimentary, promotional tickets.[132]

Attendance at games continued to rise throughout the week and so too did the number of spectators wearing the color pink. One author who attended games and later wrote a book on the tournament, reported 'the city had jumped on the Pink Power bandwagon'.[133] Civic Centre arena commentator, Brian McFarlane of Hockey Night in

Canada, reported 'the scene in Ottawa by the final game was one of pink madness. Restaurants and hotels offered "pink specials" in the form of pink drinks. Most spectators wore pink.'[134] The Team Canada coordinator was outside of the Civic Centre and commented that 'the entire street was a crowd of pink! Mothers held hands with their little girls wearing pink t-shirts. Many had faces painted pink. Some people carried pink pom-poms. Some waved pink flags. Some wore pink fake fur hats.'[135] The gold medal game between Team Canada and Team USA was nearly sold out. US president George H.W. Bush, had forwarded a letter to Team USA, urging the players to stage another 'miracle on ice', in reference to the US men's hockey team victory over the Soviet Union team at the 1980 Lake Placid Olympic Winter Games.[136] The president's letter was fixed to the glass behind the American team bench, and according to the US coach, served to motivate Team USA, whose players scored the first two goals in the game.[137] Team Canada responded with five straight goals, winning 5–2. This included a spectacular goal by Geraldine Heaney, who was checked and while airborne still managed to score.[138] Attendance at the gold medal game was reported as 8,784 spectators, the largest audience at the time to witness a women's hockey game.[139] One reporter added, 'What began with silly hype over uniform colors and lopsided preliminary games ended by winning fans with surprisingly fine hockey.'[140] Reid, who in his role as event general manager had suggested the use of the pink jerseys agreed, 'We won't have to talk about pink uniforms anymore to get people out to see women's hockey.'[141] The CAHA president added that the tournament had exceeded his expectations.[142] Team USA member Julie Andeberhan commented that the tournament organizers had done a great job marketing the event: 'We were all surprised and amused that Canada chose to wear those loud, bright pink uniforms. Everyone has their own opinion about it, but whether it's pro or con, their marketing strategy really worked.'[143]

The tournament finished with few player injuries, a result attributed to the application of the body checking/body contact rule.[144] Immediately following the gold medal game, the tournament all-star team was announced. It included Dawn McGuire (Canada) and Kelly O'Leary (US) on defense; Angela James (Canada), Cindy Curley (US) and Sari Krooks (Finland), forwards; and Tamae Satsu (Japan), goaltender. In term of media coverage of the gold medal game, it was not only reported on by the media in Canada, but internationally as well. The US-based *Sports Illustrated* used the headline 'NO PLACE FOR POM-POMS'[145]; and a *TIME Magazine International* headline read, 'The Women of Winter: An Unprecedented Ice Hockey Tournament Makes Seers Believers.'[146] Meanwhile, the headline in national Canadian magazine, *Maclean's*, read 'Equality on Ice: Women Hockey Players Win a World Profile.'[147] All three publications included a color photograph of Team Canada players in their pink and white jerseys. As IIHF tournament representative, Walter Bush, stated, 'The winner is women's hockey. This tournament has made people believers.'[148] A Toronto *Globe and Mail* article contained an interview with Walter Bush, who reported that, 'The International Ice Hockey Federation has been lobbying the International Olympic Committee to include women's hockey in the 1994 Games in Norway and chances now are "about 50–50" for 1994, and "almost certain" for 1998.'[149] IIHF president, Gunther Sabetzki, also complimented the CAHA for generating media attention for the championship, which he expressed in a telefax to the CAHA: 'In Ottawa and environs where the games were played, the CAHA as the organizer was most skilful to stimulate echo among the media, which we cannot find elsewhere.'[150] Shirley Cameron of Team Canada captured the sentiment of many players when she said, 'I hope that hockey won't be looked upon [any longer] as a man's sport, but just as a sport that men and women can play.'[151] Team Canada's

Judy Diduck would prove to be prophetic when she said, 'the young girls are going to benefit a lot from this.'[152]

The competitive and commercial success of the event established women's hockey as a legitimate elite-level sport. Several years earlier, when sport activist and scholar Bruce Kidd gave testimony in the case of Justine Blainey, a girl who was banned from playing boy's hockey in Ontario, he noted that 'women in the past have been restrained by social convention, by open ridicule, and by lack of opportunity.'[153] The 1990 WWHC gave women the opportunity to compete at the highest level, to a large audience. The caliber of play displayed in the tournament would also serve to dispel negative myths regarding the competitiveness of women's hockey.

Championship Aftermath

The event general manager commissioned a 10-minute video of game highlights of the women's championship, which he and the CAHA president took to the IIHF meeting the following month in Stockholm, Sweden, as part of the evaluation of the women's world championship as an Olympic test event.[154] Initially, the reaction of IIHF members was that 'women can't skate that fast and shoot that hard,'[155] accusing CAHA officials of having artificially accelerated the speed of the game footage.[156] After a lengthy discussion, the IIHF members conceded and agreed their president, Sabetzki, would recommend to the IOC the addition of women's hockey as a new Olympic event in the 1994 winter Olympic Games.[157]

However, it was too late for the IOC to make an acceptable arrangement with the Norwegian Olympic Organizing Committee (NOOC) for the 1994 Games.[158] The NOOC had already planned to convert their 1994 Games venues to school facilities and congress centres after the Games, and also to dismantle the wooden houses of the Olympic Village and repurpose the lumber.[159] As a result, there was little interest in constructing a new hockey arena which would have had limited use after the Games.[160] Another disincentive for the NOOC was the fact that the Norwegian Ice Hockey Association had less than 500 registered female players and their national team had placed 6th out of 8 teams at the 1990 championship.[161] On 17 November 1992, the IOC announced that women's hockey would be added to the Winter Olympic Games and it debuted in Nagano, Japan, 1998.[162] Nancy Theberge, a leading scholar of women's hockey, has argued that 'the most significant event of recent years and likely in the history of the sport is addition to the Olympic program in 1998.'[163]

The state of women's elite hockey leading up to the first women's world championship in March 1990, was still very much at a developmental level in most of Europe and in Asia, but comparatively speaking, further advanced in the US and Canada. At the time of the tournament, there were approximately 4,300 women playing in Canada. The CAHA reported that the number of registered, female, hockey players jumped 75% in the year following the 1990 women's world championship.[164] By 2013, when the world championship was again hosted in the city of Ottawa, the CAHA reported there were nearly 90,000 registered players.[165] At the 2013 tournament, former CAHA president, Murray Costello, would reminisce about the state of panic the CAHA management committee was facing as a result of the lack of interest in the 1990 championship shown by members of the media. 'At the time we were having no impact at all. No media. No ticket sales. It was crazy.'[166]

Hockey Canada paid tribute to the 1990 world championship team by having Team Canada wear replica pink and white jerseys at the 2007 world championship.[167] In

2013, the year after Costello retired from the IIHF Council, a feature article commented on how far women's hockey had come as an elite sporting spectacle. For example in 1990, world championship game tickets cost as little as $3.50 for adults, less than the cost of tickets to the Canadian women's hockey championship held the month after the world championship.[168] At the 2013 women's world championship again held in Ottawa, ticket packages for all games started at $184.[169] Where Sport Canada had contributed $50,000 of event hosting money in 1990, in 2013 Sport Canada contributed $500,000.[170] The 1990 WWHC played an instrumental role in legitimating women's hockey as an elite sport, with widespread media coverage and featuring strong athletic performances. With the support of the media, IIHF, and IOC, women's hockey would continue to grow in the decades to come.

Acknowledgments

The authors would like to thank Murray Costello, former president of the Canadian Amateur Hockey Association, Editor, Mark Dyreson, and the two anonymous reviewers for their insight and feedback on previous versions of this paper.

Disclosure statement

No potential conflict of interest was reported by the authors.

Notes

1. International Olympic Committee, 'International Olympic Committee Marketing Report, Sochi, 2014', 34, http://www.olympic.org/Documents/IOC_Marketing/Sochi_2014/LR_MktReport2014_all_Spreads.pdf (accessed 20 April 2015).
2. NBC Sports Group, 'Thursday's Women's Gold Medal Ice Hockey is Most-Streamed Game in NBC Sports Digital History, Excluding Super Bowl XLVI', NBC Sports, http://nbcsports grouppressbox.com/2014/02/20/thursdays-womens-gold-medal-ice-hockey-is-most-streamed-game-in-nbc-sports-digital-history-excluding-super-bowl-xlvi/ (accessed 15 April 2015).
3. TSN, 'TSN Scores Record Audience for the 2013 IIHF WORLD WOMEN'S CHAMPION-SHIP Gold Medal Game', Bell Media, 10 April 2013, http://www.bellmedia.ca/pr/press/tsn-scores-record-audience-for-the-2013-iihf-world-womens-championship-gold-medal-game/ (accessed 22 April 2015).
4. James Christie, 'Women's Hockey is Different', *Globe and Mail*, 8 April 2000, S-1.
5. Hockey Canada, 'Player Registration by Branch', Hockey Canada, http://www.hockey canada.ca/en-ca/Corporate/About/Annual-Report/Registration/Player-Reg (accessed 10 March 2015).
6. Carl C. Noble, *Report, in the OWHA News Update 899004*, June 1990, 9–10. Noble, vice president of administration, OWHA, reported that the 1990 number of registered players was 4,322, up 15 players from the previous season.
7. Fran Rider, *CAHA Female Council National/International Report*, 16 May 1989, 3. AHAUS reported there were 139 women's hockey teams registered in 1989, which equals 2,780 players if all teams had full rosters.

8. Nancy Theberge, Preface to *Higher Goals: Women's Ice Hockey and the Politics of Gender* (Albany: SUNY Press, 2000), ix.
9. Elizabeth Etue and Megan Williams, *On the Edge: Women Making Hockey History* (Toronto: Second Story Press, 1996).
10. These files have been in Reid's possession since the tournament was held in 1990. As per an agreement with Murray Costello, former president of the Canadian Amateur Hockey Association, the files will be sent to Hockey Canada and be made available for public use. Because the files have not yet been archived, these sources will be referenced as 'CAHA archives' throughout this paper.
11. Brian McFarlane, *Proud Past, Bright Future: One Hundred Years of Canadian Women's Hockey* (Toronto: Stoddart, 1994), 156.
12. Joanna Avery and Julie Stevens, *Too Many Men on the Ice. Women's Hockey in North America* (Victoria, BC: Polestar Book Publishers, 1997), 57.
13. Carly Adams, 'Organizing Hockey for Women: The Ladies Ontario Hockey Association and the Fight for Legitimacy, 1922–1940,' in J.C. Wong (ed.), *Coast to Coast. Hockey in Canada to the Second World War* (Toronto: University of Toronto Press, 2009), 138.
14. Ibid., 139.
15. Hockey Canada, 'About Hockey Canada: History-1 and History-2', http://www.hockey canada.ca/en-ca/Corporate/About/History/History/History-2 (accessed 10 March 2015).
16. Ibid.
17. Allan C. Hutchison and Andrew Petter, 'Private Rights/Public Wrongs: The Liberal Lie of the Charter', *University of Toronto Law Journal* 38, no. 3 (1988), 278–97.
18. Avery and Stevens, *Too Many Men*, 81.
19. Fran Rider, interview by Elizabeth Etue and M.K. Williams, *The Edge: Women Making Hockey History* (Toronto: Second Story Press, 1996), 17 July 1992, 71.
20. Mike Schroeder to Pat Reid, telefax, 9 February 1990, CAHA archives.
21. Greta L. Cohen, *Women in Sport: Issues and Controversies*, 2nd ed. (Pikesville, MD: Port City Press 2001), 19.
22. Etue and Williams, *On the Edge*; Wong, *Coast to Coast*; McFarlane, *Proud Past, Bright Future*; Avery and Stevens, *Too Many Men*; Lorna Nicholson, *Pink Power: The First Women's World Hockey Champions* (Toronto: James Lorimer and Company Ltd, 2007); Greta L. Cohen, *Women in Sport Issues and Controversies* (Oxon Hill, MD: AAHPERD Publications, 2001).
23. IIHF, 'Women's Ice Hockey on the Attack', *IIHF 1988–89 Yearbook*, 7. CAHA archives.
24. Ibid.
25. German Ice Hockey Federation to Pat Reid, telefax (n.d.). Received prior to the first game of the 1990 women's world ice hockey championship. CAHA archives.
26. Finnish Ice Hockey Federation, to Pat Reid, telefax (n.d.). Received prior to the first game of the 1990 women's world ice hockey championship. CAHA archives.
27. Rolf Schweizer to Pat Reid, telefax, Ottawa, 9 March 1990. CAHA archives.
28. *IIHF 1988–1989 Yearbook*, 8.
29. Ibid., 8.
30. Ibid., 9.
31. Ibid.
32. Ibid.
33. OWHA, '1987 World Tournament', OWHA, news release, (n.d.). CAHA archives.
34. Mark Suchman, 'Managing Legitimacy: Strategic and Institutional Approaches', *Academy of Management Review* 20 (1995), 674.
35. David Deephouse and Mark Suchman, 'Legitimacy in Organizational Institutionalism', in Royston Greenwood et al. (eds), *Sage Handbook of Organizational Institutionalism* (Los Angeles, CA: Sage, 2008), 54.
36. Mark Zwolinski, 'Canada's Hot Play Matches Uniforms', *Toronto Star*, 20 March 1990, F2.
37. FIH, 'Hockey and the FIH', http://www.fih.ch/en/fih/history (accessed 12 December 2015).
38. Lorna Nicholson, *Pink Power: The First Women's World Hockey Champions* (Toronto: James Lorimer and Company Ltd, 2007), 9; Bob Ferguson, 'High Hopes for Women's Hockey Team', *Ottawa Citizen*, 15 March 1990, F-5-6.
39. Murray Costello, email to authors, 23 February 2015.

40. Ken Whillans, Mayor of the City of Brampton, to Murray Costello, CAHA, 28 June 1989, Brampton, Ontario. CAHA archives.
41. Ferguson, 'High Hopes', F 5.
42. Deephouse and Suchman, 'Legitimacy in Organizational Institutionalism', 55.
43. Pat Reid to Abby Hoffman, Director General of Sport Canada, letter, 28 November 1989, Ottawa. CAHA archives.
44. Ibid.
45. CAHA president to CAHA officers, memorandum (n.d.), Ottawa. CAHA archives.
46. Julie Chiasson to Pat Reid, telefax, 15 September 1989, Zurich. CAHA archives.
47. Ibid.
48. Ibid.
49. Ibid.
50. German Ice Hockey Federation (DEB) to Pat Reid, telefax (n.d.). CAHA archives.
51. Frank Libera to, 'CAHA Female Council', 5 October 1989, Ottawa. CAHA archives.
52. *IIHF 1988–90 Yearbook*: 7.
53. Murray Costello report to CAHA Officers, September 1989. CAHA archives. Roman Neumayer to Murray Costello, 20 February 1990. CAHA archives.
54. *Official Program of the 1990 IIHF Women's World Ice Hockey Championship*, Ottawa, 33.
55. Theberge, *Higher Goals*, 116–26.
56. Andreas Lauer to Fran Rider, 13 April 1987, Dusseldorf. CAHA archives.
57. Etue and Williams, *On the Edge*, 273.
58. *CAHA Bulletin* 90/D10, 5 October 1989.
59. James Davidson, 'World-wide Success an Ice Goal for Women', *Toronto Star*, 19 March 1990, C2.
60. Ibid.
61. Michael Landsberg commentary, TSN coverage of the Canada-Sweden game, 19 March 1990. CAHA archives.
62. Etue and Williams, *On the Edge*, 272.
63. Murray Costello to the CAHA Officers, memorandum, September 1989. CAHA archives.
64. Official IIHF sign off sheet confirming teams and the schedule for the first women's world ice hockey championship, 14 September 1989. CAHA archives.
65. Pat Reid to Murray, 12 September 1989. CAHA archives.
66. Roman Neumayer to Murray Costello, 22 September 1989. CAHA archives.
67. Pat Reid to Sue Neill, 25 October 1989, Ottawa. CAHA archives.
68. Frank Libera to Abby Hoffman, 30 October 1989, Ottawa. CAHA archives.
69. Ibid.
70. Roman Neumayer to Murray Costello, 22 September 1989. CAHA archives.
71. Cesar W. Luthi to Murray Costello, 4 December 1989. CAHA archives.
72. Pat Reid to Murray Costello, 12 September 1990. CAHA archives.
73. Rick Brace (TSN) to Pat Reid, 12 October 1990. CAHA archives.
74. Angela Spicer to Pat Reid, 19 February 1990. CAHA archives.
75. Ibid.
76. OWHA sponsorship package for the 1987 OWHA world tournament (n.d.), Toronto. CAHA archives.
77. Angela Spicer to Pat Reid, 19 February 1990, Ottawa. CAHA archives.
78. Murray Costello to Mike Morgan (CBC), Jim Thompson (TSN) and Gary Maavara (CTV) 16 October 1989. CAHA archives. For an overview of the relationship between the CAHA and Hockey Canada, see Julie Stevens, 'The Canadian Hockey Association Merger and the Emergence of the Amateur Sport Enterprise,' *Journal of Sport Management* 20, no. 1 (2006), 74.
79. Pat Reid to Murray Costello, 25 July 1989. CAHA archives.
80. Frank Libera to WWIHC committee members, 27 October 1989. CAHA archives.
81. Memorandum of Understanding between Her Majesty the Queen in Right in Canada as represented by the Minister of State for Fitness and Amateur Sport and the Canadian Amateur Hockey Association, 6 February 1990. CAHA archives.
82. Ibid.
83. Ibid.
84. Ibid.

85. Jan-Ake Edvinsson to Murray Costello, 14 March 1990. CAHA archives.
86. Pat Reid to Abby Hoffman, 18 June 1990. CAHA archives.
87. Don Cherry is a commentator who appears during the intermission of 'Hockey Night in Canada' telecasts. He is at times a polarizing figure due to his outspokenness on contentious topics (including women in sport). To give an example of his popularity, a CBC program that aired in 2004 found Cherry to be ranked seventh in a poll to determine the 'Greatest Canadian'.
88. In a telephone conversation with Reid on 14 March 1990, Don Cherry agreed to promote Team Canada at the first women's world ice hockey championship in Ottawa. Cherry forgot to do the promotion that night but did do a brief promotion 24 March 1990 during 'Hockey Night in Canada'.
89. Pat Reid to Mike Barnett, president CorpSport International, 8 September 1989. CAHA archives.
90. Michael G. Barnett to Pat Reid, 11 September 1989. CAHA archives.
91. Ringette Canada, '1990 World Ringette Championship', http://www.ringette.ca/event_re sults/1990-world-ringette-championship-gloucester-ontario-canada (accessed 30 October 2015).
92. CAHA press release, 13 March 1990. CAHA archives.
93. Ibid.
94. Wayne Scanlan, 'Ice Women Cometh', *Ottawa Citizen*, 6 March 1990, E-5.
95. Kevin Allen, 'Olympics is the Ultimate Goal for Women's Hockey; US Women's Hockey Schedule', *USA Today*, 19 March 1990, C3.
96. Ferguson, 'High Hopes', F5.
97. *Official Program, 1990 Women's World Ice Hockey Championship,* 21. CAHA archives.
98. John MacKinnon, 'Female Worlds Prove a Point', *Ottawa Citizen*, 25 March 1990, B1.
99. Scanlan, 'Ice Women Cometh', E5.
100. Murray Costello to the Ice Hockey Federations of Sweden, Japan and West Germany, telefax, 16 October 1989. CAHA archives.
101. Ibid.
102. Pat Reid to Mauri Nylund, president Tackla, 1 February 1990. CAHA archives.
103. TSN video tapes of the four TSN televised games: 19 March 1990 Canada versus Sweden; 24 March 1990 Canada versus Finland; 25 March 1990 Finland versus Sweden, and Canada versus USA. Author's collection. Copies of games can be obtained directly from TSN by contacting audiencerelations@tsn.ca.
104. Nicholson, *Pink Power*, 46.
105. Ibid.
106. Wayne Scanlan, 'A Hockey Life', *Ottawa Citizen*, 31 October 2012, B4.
107. Nicholson, *Pink Power*, 46.
108. Ibid., 44.
109. Scanlan, 'A Hockey Life', B4.
110. Nicholson, *Pink Power*, 46.
111. Scanlan, 'A Hockey Life', B4.
112. Dave McMaster, 'Final report', 22 July 1990. CAHA archives.
113. McCrae, 'Team Canada: Stereotype or High Fashion?', 9.
114. Parliament Hill is the name given to the land where Canadian Parliament sits.
115. Scanlan, 'Ice Women Cometh', E5.
116. Roy MacGregor, 'Fast-Growing Women's Game has Become the "Pinnacle of Hockey"', *Globe and Mail*, 12 March 1990, S6.
117. Jane O'Hara, 'Sorry Girls Pink Stinks', *Ottawa Sun*, 18 March 1990, C-1.
118. McCrae, 'Team Canada: Stereotype or High Fashion?', B1, 8.
119. Ibid., 9.
120. Scanlan, 'A Hockey Life', B4.
121. James Davidson, '"On Top of the World": Jubilant Women Say After Capturing Gold', *Special to the Globe and Mail*, 26 March 1990, C4.
122. Canadian Press, 'Pink Power Rules Rink at Tourney', *Edmonton Journal*, 22 March 1990, D2.
123. Wayne Scanlan, 'Breaking the Ice: James Helping to Establish Women's Hockey at Worlds', *Ottawa Citizen,* 22 March 1990, D 9.

124. Janet Brooks, 'Powerful in Pink', *Champion* 14, no. 1 (1990), 46.
125. Nolan Zavoral, 'The Puck Doesn't Stop Here for Female Players: Article and Interview with IIHF Delegate to the Women's World Hockey Championship, Walter Bush', *Star-Tribune Newspaper of the Twin Cities Mpls.-St. Paul*, Metro, 18 March 1990, 18C.
126. Jan-Ake Edvinsson to Murray Costello, 6 March 1990. CAHA archives.
127. Women's World Ice Hockey Championship Opening Ceremonies, Report (n.d.). CAHA archives.
128. *Official program of the 1990 IIHF women's world ice hockey championship*, March 1990, 21. CAHA archives.
129. Official IIHF women's world ice hockey championship game sheet, Japan vs. Germany, Barbara Ann Scott Arena, Monday, 19 March 1990, 13:00. CAHA archives.
130. Ibid.
131. John McKinnon, 'Female Worlds Prove a Point', B1.
132. Wayne Scanlan, 'Canada Wins Big; Buries Sweden in Opener Team Canada 15, Sweden 1', *Ottawa Citizen*, 20 March 1990, C1.
133. Nicholson, *Pink Power*, 91.
134. McFarlane, *Proud Past, Bright Future*, 156. 'Hockey Night in Canada' has become a cultural institution, airing on Saturday nights on CBC for over 60 years.
135. Nicholson, *Pink Power*, 93.
136. Wayne Scanlan, 'Women's World Championship: We Win!; Canada Beats Early Jitters to Crush US in Front of 8,724', *Ottawa Citizen*, 26 March 1990, E1.
137. James Davidson, 'On Top of the World', C4.
138. Ibid.
139. Nicholson, *Pink Power*, 97.
140. Scanlan, 'Women's World Championship', E1.
141. Ibid.
142. MacKinnon, 'Female Worlds Prove a Point', B1.
143. Avery and Stevens, *Too Many Men,* 163.
144. James Davidson, 'Limelight Dazes Delighted Players at Women's Event', *Special to the Globe and Mail*, 24 March 1990, A18. Previous literature has claimed that there were numerous injuries at the tournament, attributed to the fact that body checking was allowed. This was not the case, as referees called penalties for body checking during the tournament. Etue and Willams, *On the Edge,* 272.
145. Paul Fichtenbaum, 'No Place for Pom-Poms: The Tough US Women were Second in the First Worlds', *Sports Illustrated*, 2 April 1990, 59.
146. Sally B. Donnelly, 'The Women of Winter: An Unprecedented Ice Hockey Tournament Makes Seers Believers', *TIME Magazine International*, 9 April 1990, 67.
147. Jenish D'Arcy, Sharon Doyle Driedger, and Bruce Garrioch, 'Equality on Ice: Women Hockey Players Win a World Profile', *Maclean's*, 2 April 1990, 58.
148. Ibid., 67.
149. James Davidson, 'Women's Hockey Intent on Escaping Obscurity', *Special to Globe and Mail*, 26 March 1990, C4.
150. Gunther Sabetzki to Murray Costello (n.d.). CAHA archives.
151. Ibid.
152. Canadian Press, 'Another Sensational Granato is Tony's High-Scoring Sister', *Toronto Star*, 24 March 1990, SA2.
153. Doug Beardsley, *Country on Ice* (Winlaw, BC: Polestar Press, 1987), 117.
154. Davidson, 'Women's Hockey Intent on Escaping Obscurity', C4.
155. Roy MacGregor, 'Fast-Growing Women's Game Has Become "the Pinnacle of Hockey"', *Globe and Mail*, 12 March 2013, S1.
156. Ibid.
157. MacKinnon, 'Female Worlds Prove a Point', B1.
158. Jean-Loup Chappelet, 'Olympic Environmental Concerns as a Legacy of the Winter Games', *The International Journal of the History of Sport* 25, no. 14 (2008), 1884–1902.
159. Ibid.
160. Ibid.
161. Official results, 1990 IIHF women's world ice hockey championship (n.d.). CAHA archives.

162. Avery and Stevens, *Too Many Men*, 36.
163. Theberge, *Higher Goals*, 17.
164. McFarlane, *Proud Past, Bright Future,* 156.
165. Scanlan, 'A Hockey Life', B4.
166. Ibid.
167. Randy Starkman, 'Sunohara to Get Last Laugh as Canadians Think Pink; Veteran the Only Player Left From 1990 Team Being Honoured To-Night', *Toronto Star*, 7 April 2007, C6.
168. CAHA press release #001, 'National Women's Hockey Championships' (n.d.). CAHA archives.
169. Scanlan, 'A Hockey Life', B4.
170. Rachel Brady, 'Women's World Hockey Championship Returns to Ottawa with New Identity', *Globe and Mail*, 1 April 2013, C1.

Region and Race: The Legacies of the St Louis Olympics

Mark Dyreson ⓘ

St Louis staged the third modern Olympics in 1904, an event most historians have labelled as a less than memorable occasion and some have contended nearly derailed the nascent Olympic movement. Consigned to a regional hamlet rather than a global city, the 1904 St Louis games were supposedly a model of how not to conduct an Olympian spectacle. Taking a different perspective, however, the St Louis games had a profound influence on how the United States has staged Olympics. The Olympics have not been held in established or well-known American metropolises but have consistently gone to up-and-coming cities in border regions eager to make national and global reputations. In addition, the 1904 St Louis games were held in a legally segregated city but permitted the inclusion for the first time of African-American athletes in Olympic competition. Race and region provided foundations for American interpretations of the 1904 Olympics and have remained paramount in national memories of Olympian events ever since. From St Louis in 1904 through Atlanta in 1996 race and region have been central themes in American Olympic experiences.

Historians have already spilled a considerable amount of ink on the 1904 St Louis Olympics. They have analysed the intersections of nationhood, social class, and ethnic and racial categorization that collided at the Games of the IIIrd Olympiad of the modern era.[1] They have interrogated the infamous spectacle of 'Anthropology Days' where anthropologists and athletic officials bet on the prospect of whether or not a collection of so-called 'primitives' housed in various exhibits at the exposition that also sheltered the Olympics could best the performances of so-called 'civilized' athletes.[2] Some researchers have interpreted 'Anthropology Days' not as a strange aberration in the history of modern sport but rather one episode in a long series of allegedly scientific tests of racial prowess at the Olympics and in other athletic venues.[3] Revisionists have asserted that the connection of the Olympic movement to the World's Fair movement was far deeper and more complex than most scholars understood and that St Louis did not represent the end of the alliance between the two institutions.[4] Some recent chroniclers have also sought to revise the all-to-prevalent dismissal of the St Louis games as an unmitigated disaster that nearly destroyed the nascent Olympic movement and required the creation of a special 'intercalated' Olympics by Baron Pierre de Coubertin and the International Olympic Committee (IOC) two years later in Athens in order to resurrect the endeavour from the misguided designs of parochial Americans.[5]

While historians have cultivated their gardens, the St Louis games have faded almost entirely from public memory. Very little visible legacy remains from the St

Louis Olympics. An archaeologically-minded visitor to contemporary St Louis would be hard-pressed to find architectural traces of the games. Some of the venues were temporary sites erected on the grounds of the World's·Fair – itself an amalgam of mostly temporary structures. The stadium where the games took place, built in 1902 on the campus of Washington University, remains and has reverted to its originally intended purpose. It currently hosts football games at Washington University, an elite academic institution with an athletic programme that plays at the small-college level and draws crowds that number (on good days) in the 100s and not in the 10s of 1,000s that gather for 'big time' college football on some other American campuses.[6]

Most of the small number of annual visitors to this tiny venue – one of the earliest reinforced concrete athletic structures built in the US – remain blissfully unaware that it once housed the Olympics. Only a small and difficult to find sign marks it as an Olympic edifice. Francis Stadium, named after the civic luminary who ran the world's fair in St Louis, hardly retains the Olympic cachet of Beijing's 'Bird Nest' or Berlin's iconic remnant of the 1936 'Nazi' Olympics or even the Los Angeles Coliseum, a two-time stage for the Olympian spectacles.[7] The refurbished Panatheniac stadium that housed the first modern Olympics in 1896 serves as a major tourist attraction for Athens – not quite the Parthenon but still one of the temples of 'antiquity' (or its neo-ancient reproductions) visited in vast numbers by pilgrims to the shrines of Western civilization.[8] Francis Stadium, by contrast, attracts only a tiny handful of curious Olympiophiles.

Not only in global popular culture but even in American popular culture the St Louis games are the 'forgotten' Olympics, overshadowed by Los Angeles and Atlanta, and even by Lake Placid, Salt Lake City, and Squaw Valley. In fact, Americans forgot that St Louis housed the first Olympics on their native soil rather quickly. Only a few decades later, the publicity brochure produced by the Southern Pacific railroad to entice tourists to travel its trains to the 1932 Los Angeles games failed to acknowledge St Louis had ever staged an Olympian spectacle. The flyer proclaimed that the 'Los Angeles Games will mark the first time that this great international sports event has ever been held in the United States.'[9] Decades later, *Life Magazine* recalled the event by wryly observing that 'the heartland put on a homegrown – and unremembered – Olympics.'[10] As recently as the centennial of the St Louis spectacle in 2004 a local historian, Sharon Smith of the Missouri Historical Society, lamented: 'It's a frustrating thing: You go to Los Angeles and you know the Olympics were held there … Here there is no Walk of Fame or plaques.'[11]

Especially annoying to the handful of curators of Olympic heritage who want the 1904 St Louis games to seize a larger role in the national imagination is the fact that the events witnessed the first participation of African-American athletes in an Olympics.[12] Given the centrality of race in American narratives about the Olympics in particular and sport in general, the erasure of St Louis from nation's Olympic recollections seems even more glaring. For several generations of Americans perhaps the two most iconic moments that focus their Olympic memories are Jesse Owens' 'triumph' in 1936 over Adolf Hitler and Nazi racial ideology and the black-gloved salutes of John Carlos and Tommy Smith on the medal stand at Mexico City in 1968.[13]

Race, always at the nexus of 'American dilemmas,' and region, the backwaters of the American 'heartland,' reside at the core of the legacies that the St Louis Olympics have bequeathed to faded national memories. Though St Louis might be almost forgotten in American Olympic history, the intersections of region and race first revealed in St Louis have shaped and continue to influence American engagement in the Olympics. These twin legacies, originally manifested in St Louis, have for more than a century shaped what types of American cities have hosted the Olympics and propelled struggles over the paradoxes of racial segregation and racial inclusion into the centre of American Olympic narratives.

The legacy of location marks a good starting point for fleshing out these twin narratives. In the history of hosting the summer incarnations of the modern games almost every region or nation has designated its most important urban centre as the Olympic site.[14] Ponder the list for a moment: Athens, Paris, London, Stockholm, Berlin (cancelled), Antwerp, Paris again, Amsterdam, Berlin again, Tokyo (cancelled), London again, Helsinki, Melbourne, Rome, Tokyo again, Mexico City, Montreal, Moscow, Seoul, Barcelona, Sydney, Athens again, Beijing, London for the third time, and now on to Rio de Janeiro and then to Tokyo once again. The cities on this list are generally the largest in their nations or close rivals in terms of population and influence. They are the economic and cultural capitals of their nations and mainly the political capitals as well – or, like Barcelona in Spain and Montreal in Canada they represent the dreamed of capitals of proto-nations embedded uncomfortably in older political constellations. Winter games might go to ski resorts or quaint villages or smaller cities looking to draw snow-seeking tourists but the summer games gravitate to the most important and influential global cities.[15]

The cities left out of this litany reveal important exceptions to this pattern. In 1972 West Germany staged the Olympics in Munich. Hardly a German hamlet, West German leaders selected their nation's third largest city precisely because Munich was not Berlin and they did not want to remind the globe of the infamous 1936 'Nazi Olympics.'[16] The rest of missing cities on the list are in the United States. Indeed, the US has hosted more Olympic summer games than any other nation, from St Louis in 1904 to Los Angeles in 1932 and 1984 to Atlanta in 1996. The American Olympic cities represent a striking departure from the typical hosting tradition. They are not the nation's capital nor are they, from the perspective of American urban history, old and long-settled centres of commerce of culture. The original triumvirate of American metropolises that fit alongside the typical Olympic hosts, Boston, Philadelphia, and New York has never hosted an Olympics. New York and Philadelphia have made a few half-hearted efforts over a century to acquire the games. Boston finally entered the fray recently only to quickly withdraw from the challenge.[17]

Historically, the Olympics staged in the US have gone to rapidly expanding cities situated in the borderlands between regions that have been symbols of American expansionism. St Louis in 1904 represented a dynamic new hub, having just jumped past Boston into fourth place on the list of the nation's largest cities behind New York, Chicago, and Philadelphia.[18] Chicagoans mightily resented that St Louis boosters managed to relocate the 1904 Olympics from their city to the Louisiana Purchase Exposition but as a celebration of American exceptionalism and expansionism the move in retrospect makes a great deal of sense.[19] Los Angeles in 1932 also represented a rapidly growing hub, having come out of nowhere in the previous decades to clamber past St Louis and Cleveland into fifth place on the list of largest cities behind New York, Chicago, Philadelphia, and Detroit. Like St Louis, Los Angeles represented another 'gateway to the West,' an urban sign of exceptionalism and expansionism.[20] By 1984 Los Angeles was in the process of superseding Chicago for second place on the list and fit more comfortably with the likes of Rome and Tokyo on the list of global cities – but at that point the rest of urban areas in the world had decided that the Olympics were worthless 'white elephants' and not a single foreign city bid against the

'City of Angels' – with the exception of Teheran that launched a preliminary proposal that quickly unravelled as Iran began its immersion into the cauldrons of revolution.[21] Los Angeles remained in the 1980s a 'gateway,' a key locus of American visions of exceptionalism and expansion and a portal to the vast swaths of globe – as the infamous title of the journalist David Rieff's book, *Los Angeles: Capital of the Third World* (1991) trenchantly observed.[22]

In 1996 when Atlanta garnered the centennial celebration of the Olympics, much to the chagrin of Greeks who dreamed of returning the games to their modern roots in Athens and were incensed that an American city that merely possessed a Greek name had grabbed the prize, the hub of the 'New South' was clambering toward 11th place amongst the largest US metropolitan areas, hardly a position comparable to Beijing or even to Athens.[23] Atlanta stood in late twentieth-century American culture as another emblem of exceptionalism and expansion, as it had stood since the late nineteenth century when it was known as the 'gate city to the New South.' One hundred years later the old 'gate city' was along with Los Angeles one of the capitals of the new 'Sun-Belt' driving American commerce, culture, and politics with a global reach into the emerging markets of Africa, Asia, and Latin America.[24]

What emerges from a consideration of where the Olympics have been celebrated in the United States then is a clear pattern. The Olympics have gone not to the metropolitan core of the ancient, by American standards, Eastern Establishment such as Philadelphia, New York, or Boston. Instead, Olympic sites have been located in the gleaming new cities of the American frontier – whether in the historical frontier of westward expansion signified by St Louis and later by Los Angeles, and in Atlanta, a city that in the 1990s represented a key American outpost in the new global economy, a metropolitan leader in the rise of the Sunbelt to national leadership, and an emerging centre of the reincorporation of the American South into the mainstream of national life.[25]

This tradition makes the United States unique as an Olympic host. Imagine Brazil staging the 2016 Olympics not in Rio but in the hinterlands of Amazonian rainforest, in flood-choked Manaus – and recall the negative publicity Brazil received from staging 2014 World Cup games there.[26] Or imagine that China had decided to celebrate the 2008 Olympics not in Beijing but at Ürümqi, a city of three million located on the isolated Mongolian steppes of western China. That such a pipedream never took hold in China or Brazil but has dominated the Olympic experiences of the United States offers a significant contrast to the meaning of Olympic productions in American culture as opposed to the rest of the world.

The legacy of St Louis thus stretches across the whole of the twentieth century and illuminates the incorporation of new regions into the American power structure. When Olympic spectacles came to the United States they went not to the traditional, established power centres that had dominated the first phases of the urban revolution but to up-and-coming cities that wanted to make their marks on the national and international landscape. Given that the most important entities in making the decisions about which cities hosted American games, the American Olympic Committee (AOC) and the Amateur Athletic Union (AAU), had their headquarters and drew the vast majority of their leadership in the first half of the twentieth century from New York, Boston, and Philadelphia, or from the emerging titan of the upper Middle West, Chicago, and the outcome of the selection process is in many ways even more surprising.[27]

The second legacy that St Louis contributed to American Olympic history is also connected to regionalism in the United States. The St Louis Olympics witnessed the first appearance of African-American competitors in an Olympic stadium. Their debut, in a city with racial customs shaped by legalized segregation, highlights the tensions and paradoxes embedded in post-Reconstruction US racial policies. Region represented a key component in the complex racial tapestries that varied from place to place across the nation. From the 1904 St Louis Olympics through 1996 Atlanta Olympics race and region shaped the narratives that emerged from American games.

The organizers of the St Louis fair and Olympics insisted that they drew no colour lines at any of their venues, an unsupportable claim in a deeply and legally segregated city that manifested a strong sympathy for Southern stances on racial issues. On the other hand, St Louis marked the first appearance of African-American athletes in an Olympic competition. The city would open the gates of its Olympic stadium to integrated national athletic championships on numerous occasions after the 1904 Olympics hosting championship meets in 1917, 1954, and 1963 that contributed to long-standing rhetorical claims that selection processes for US Olympic teams never drew colour lines. In American culture, the Olympics have since 1904 harboured narratives about the nature and limits of racial inclusion and exclusion in national life, a St Louis legacy that produced one of the most powerful moments of the 1996 Atlanta games when an ailing Muhammad Ali memorably lit the torch to launch a games held in a city that had paradoxically been a stronghold of the Confederacy and a bastion of fealty to segregation but had also been the Southern capital of the Civil Rights Movement.[28]

Indeed, Atlanta proved a controversial choice not only for beating Athens out of the centennial Olympics but also since as many observers both in the US and beyond contended at the time, for staging an Olympics for the first time in the American South. The editors of the *Christian Science Monitor* proclaimed after Atlanta's winning bid that '[i]t will be the first Olympiad held in the American South and the first summer games ever held in the United States east of the Mississippi River,' adding that 'the urgency to bring it all off successfully is as palpable as a summer thunderstorm.'[29] A host of other media outlets played up the first Southern Olympics angle. From Los Angeles, host of two other American Olympic spectacles, came the caution that the '1996 Games are the first in the American South and promise to give Atlanta both glory and headaches.'[30]

While the *Christian Science Monitor*'s assertion that Atlanta staged the first Olympics east of the Mississippi River was geographically accurate since the site for the 1904 Olympics resided just a few miles west of the Mississippi's broad expanse, the historical contention that Atlanta was the first Southern city to host the Olympics is a bit more debatable. St Louis stands as a regional conundrum. Boosters, critics, and scholars have routinely debated the proper cultural location for the city, labelling it variously as a colonial outpost of the Eastern Establishment core of Boston, New York, and Philadelphia, or as a Western boomtown like Denver, Kansas City, or Portland, or as a Midwestern metropolis akin to Chicago, Minneapolis, and Indianapolis.[31] A few historians have even identified it a Southern city, noting its historic connections to New Orleans and the deeper South, to the cotton kingdoms, and to slavery and its successor systems of racial oppression. True, Missouri did not secede during the Civil War and St Louis remained a relatively stalwart stronghold of Union support but the South's boundaries have long been murkier than the old bifurcation of the Mason-Dixon Line or the dotted lines of the Confederacy on Civil War maps reveal. In a myriad ways, from music to cuisine to migration patterns to racial sentiments, the South extends into St Louis. While seeking to avoid a fight with those who would label St Louis a borderland between the East and West, any critical chronicler of St Louis would concede that the

'Gateway City' has a portal that opens to Dixie and that traffic runs through that doorway in both directions. St Louis stands as the staging point for the opening of the American West but it also served as an urban bastion of the peculiar institution, the place where Dred Scott began his quixotic quest to assert his right to emancipation and where in his years of bondage William Wells Brown sold out a fellow slave for a dollar in order to escape a jailer's lashing.[32]

The Louisiana Purchase Exposition that brought the world to St Louis in 1904 and provided a starring role for the third instalment of the modern Olympics in the fair sought to brand the city as Western metropolis and explicitly ignored the connections between the 'Gateway City' and the South. David R. Francis, the former mayor of St Louis, governor of Missouri, and US Secretary of the Interior who helmed the Louisiana Purchase Exposition Company that ran the world's fair, boasted in his official report that his American production had achieved a 'distinct universality and democracy' that surpassed all previous incarnations of these international gatherings. Francis contended that his fair was free from racial discrimination. 'All were entered upon an equal footing,' Francis insisted. 'No line was drawn by segregation or special treatment of any kind,' he proclaimed. Francis maintained that in every venue in the fair '[a]ll were set upon the plane of even competition, for this was a thorough and comprehensive test' of the skills of the competing nations.[33]

The realities of racial intercourse at the St Louis Fair did not, of course, match Francis' flowery hyperbole. Racial barriers flourished at the fair and African-American visitors reported a wide range of hostile actions, not the least of which was the cancellation of a 'Negro Day' at the exposition. A 'Daughters of the Confederacy Day,' in contrast, went off without a hitch.[34] Still, in the narrow confines of the Olympic track and field meet at David R. Francis Stadium, named after the exposition's helmsman, on the segregated campus of Washington University African-American athletes competed for the first time in Olympic competition. George Poage, a hurdler for the University of Wisconsin and the Milwaukee Athletic Club, won two bronze medals. Joseph Stadler, a standing high jumper and standing triple jumper (now discontinued events) for Cleveland's Franklin Athletic Club, earned a bronze and a silver medal.[35]

The St Louis Olympics consolidated a tradition which held that racial boundaries should not directly intrude into the upper echelons of American track and field even if they could be easily discerned in many places right beyond the narrow confines of the stadium.[36] From St Louis forward the organizers of American track and field teams for the Olympics, for Olympic trials to select US teams, as well as for national championship meets that showcased Olympic talents, scrupulously maintained that no colour lines be permitted in their events, even when they held them in cities such as St Louis where legal segregation flourished. This does not mean that the AAU or the AOC (rechristened at the United States Olympic Committee after the Second World War) should be valorized as historic citadels of integration, inclusion, or enlightenment.[37] To the contrary, like many national organizations these groups represented an amalgam of regional collectives, each with their own regional racial policies and sensibilities. Some of the branches permitted blacks to join as individuals, as members of black clubs, or even as members of integrated clubs. Other branches, most notoriously the Southern Association headquartered in New Orleans, practiced rigid segregation.[38]

The resulting hotchpotch of colour lines and racial attitudes characterized not only the AAU and AOC but a diverse spectrum of other national bodies, from the alliances of mainline Protestant denominations to the Democratic Party. Like other national umbrella groups that vested considerable autonomy in their regional units and lacked an explicit national policy on 'race questions,' the patchwork of racial traditions often created crises at national events. In the era from the end of Reconstruction during which *de jure* as well as de facto segregation rapidly advanced, the price of 'national harmony' frequently required the sacrifice of African-American civil rights.[39]

In one particular aspect, however, the AAU and the AOC were remarkably consistent and remarkably progressive. While the top echelon of leadership remained 'lily white' into the later stages of the twentieth century and it routinely tolerated with little dissent racial exclusion in regional branches, the AAU scrupulously practiced racial inclusion at its most prestigious events, the national track and field championships, the Olympic trials, and on American Olympic teams.[40] The St Louis Olympics at which Poage and Stadler competed also served as the AAU national championships. Poage's performances helped his Milwaukee Athletic Club secure a third place finish behind the New York Athletic Club and the Chicago Athletic Association in the Olympian contest for AAU club supremacy.[41]

The AAU track and field championships in that era ranked in American sporting imaginations just a step below the Olympics. Cities with Olympic aspirations vied to host the national meets to polish their national pedigrees and to bolster their Olympic prospects.[42] Just three years after the St Louis Olympics another world's fair, the tri-centennial celebration in 1907 of the founding of Jamestown, brought the AAU championship meet to Norfolk in the heart of the Jim Crow South.[43] The superlative African-American quarter-miler John B. Taylor won the AAU national title for his specialty in Virginia, the first national title earned by a black athlete. Though some AAU clubs from Richmond and Norfolk boycotted the meet over the inclusion of Taylor and a handful of other black athletes,[44] the AAU leadership held firm on its policy of refusing to draw colour lines in the competition even as they permitted segregation in the grandstands. When rumours swirled that the AAU was considering drawing a colour line in future championships, *The Freeman*, an African-American newspaper in Indianapolis assured readers that these stories were groundless. *The Freeman*'s source, 'a man in high A.A.U. authority,' proclaimed: 'There has never been any such discrimination in our sports, nor will there be – a good amateur, whether black or white, will always have the same footing in the A.A.U. field.'[45]

At least on the field that pronouncement proved accurate. In 1914 the AAU awarded segregated Baltimore the championships. Brooklyn's Smart Set Athletic Club, one of the first black athletic associations in the nation, sent a five-man contingent to the event. Several African Americans, including some Smart Set stars, placed highly in open competition with whites.[46] Three years later the national meet returned to St Louis. Staged just months after the one of the nation's most destructive and deadly race riots rocked East St Louis, just across the Mississippi River from St Louis, the meet drew several African-American stars including contingents from the Alpha Physical Culture Club and the Salem Crescent Athletic Association, black clubs from New York City.[47]

In both Baltimore and St Louis white urban boosters accepted integrated competition as the price segregated cities were required to pay for attracting the high-profile track meets. Outside of the stadium floor – even in the stands – the legal strictures and customary practices underpinning segregation remained intact. The only city that seriously pushed back against AAU racial policy for championship meets was New Orleans, the fortress of the rigidly segregated Southern Association. AAU and AOC leaders who were eager to curry favour with the Southern Association and spread interest in track and field to the South hoped to avoid direct confrontations over the issue when in 1910 they granted New Orleans the national championships.

The sports editor of the *New Orleans Times Picayune* did not take the cue and threw down the racial gauntlet to the national AAU. 'The surest way to ruin the good results of the A.A.U.'s work in the South would be to allow the smart Mr James E. Sullivan, secretary-treasurer of the A.A.U., to use some of the funds sent him by New Orleans in paying the expenses of a big team of Eastern athletes that contained a negro or two,' warned the correspondent.[48]

A potential confrontation fizzled when no African-American athletes applied to enter the New Orleans meet. The great quarter-miler John Taylor who had won an AAU national crown in 1907 at Norfolk and a year later became the first African American to earn an Olympic gold medal as a member of the victorious 4×400 m relay at the 1908 London games would certainly have challenged American track leaders to live up to their promise to prevent segregated cities from drawing colour lines at AAU meets. Tragically, Taylor contracted typhoid fever on the voyage back from London and passed away in December of 1908. No other African-American athletes or clubs entered the 1910 championships and so New Orleans and the AAU avoided a showdown.[49]

In 1927 when the AAU once again awarded New Orleans the event confrontation proved inevitable. Unlike 1910, it was clear that African-American competitors would seek to enter the New Orleans meet this time around, in particular William DeHart Hubbard, the defending Olympic and national champion in the long jump. Early reports from the 'Crescent City' indicated that New Orleans would bend its segregation system to allow black athletes to compete against whites.[50] That deal soon unravelled as the mayor and officials of the Southern AAU revealed they were planning to bar African American participants.[51] AAU leaders reacted swiftly. Frederick Rubien, the national secretary-treasurer, declared to the media that the 'Amateur Athletic Union, being a national and patriotic body, has no right to bar any man from its game because of race or creed.' Rubien regretted that New Orleans took a hard line on the colour line. 'I had hoped that such a stand never would be taken in America,' he lamented. 'Negroes in the past have competed for the United States in the Olympic games abroad and have won high honors there,' Rubien reminded the nation. 'What a strange situation to refuse them the right to compete in the national games of their own country,' he concluded.[52]

The AAU stripped the event from New Orleans and transferred the 1927 meet to Lincoln, Nebraska.[53] Southern cities that wanted to polish their images with prestigious national track championships recognized that they would not be able to exclude blacks from the events. Dallas, Texas, envious of the success of Southwestern rival Los Angeles in branding its urban identity with the Olympics in 1932, launched a campaign to garner a national championship and a US Olympic trial with ambitions to someday in the nearer rather than the distant future launch an Olympic bid. Texan sport officials bolted from the segregated Southern AAU and launched a new and integrated Southwestern branch of the AAU. They then set out to garner the 1936 US Olympic trials as a highlight of their 1936 centennial celebration. They failed in that endeavour but managed to get Eddie Tolan and Ralph Metcalfe, the African-American sprint stars of the 1932 Los Angeles Olympics, to appear in an AAU-sanctioned meet at the Centennial Fair in the Cotton Bowl, the first integrated sporting event in Texas.[54] A year later many of the black stars of the US Olympic track team from the 1936 Berlin Olympics competed in the 1937 Pan American Olympics in Dallas. A handful of black athletes from Latin America also appeared. In both these events the erasure of colour lines did not extend beyond the floor of the Cotton Bowl. Black fans sat in segregated sections of the stadium and black athletes, both foreign and domestic, were consigned to separate housing and eating accommodations.[55]

In 1946 the AAU national meet returned to the Texas when San Antonio won the bidding to host. By this time the context of racial debates regarding African-American participation had changed quite a bit. Black athletes, clubs, and journalists, and many of their white supporters, were ready to challenge colour lines not just inside of stadiums but in the grandstands and the surrounding communities as well. Many of them threatened to boycott San Antonio not over the prospect of a colour line – a boundary that white San Antonio boosters had already promised not to draw – that would keep blacks out of the meet but on the grounds that black athletes should not be subjected to Jim Crow conditions in host cities. Some black and white advocates of integration offered an alternative view, arguing that staging integrated meets in cities such as San Antonio would spur progress toward civil rights in other social arenas. The AAU sided with adherents of the latter position.[56]

Before the burgeoning Civil Rights Movement of the 1950s and 1960s finally tore down the scaffolding of legal segregation in the United States, the AAU awarded the national championship event to other segregated cities, College Park, Maryland in 1950, and St Louis in both 1954 and 1963.[57] Black athletes competed in St Louis in both the year that the *Brown v. the Board of Education* decision overturned the pernicious fiction of the 'separate but equal doctrine' and in the year that the armies of the Civil Rights Movement staged the March on Washington and heard Martin Luther King, Jr's 'I Have a Dream Speech.' Integrated competition in St Louis had not yet eradicated segregation in many places. However, the end of colour lines not only on American playing fields and cinder tracks but in most other realms was in sight. The legacy of racial inclusion in elite track and field competitions that began at 1904 in St Louis Olympics contributed to the victory by producing a variety of racial narratives that challenged colour lines in different regions of the nation.

In the early 1970s, as battles over legal segregation ended and the United States entered a new era of debates over the meaning of race, seven American cities considered entering a bid for the 1984 Olympics. It had become clear by 1977 that one of the seven would garner the bid as not a single other city in the world wanted the games after Teheran, descending into the maelstrom of the Islamic Revolution, dropped out the competition. One city, St Louis, never got its bid off the drawing board.[58] Three of the American cities pulled out of the race after the initial round, including Boston, Chicago, and Atlanta. New York City and Los Angeles remained strong contenders, along with New Orleans which had by then become a major site for American sporting spectacles such as the Super Bowl and wanted to step up to an international event. Los Angeles eventually won the race and hosted the 1984 Olympics.[59] Atlanta would garner its games in 1996. In all of those venues the legacies of region and race that since 1904 had shaped American Olympic affairs remained powerful features in their quest to join the list of Olympic cities. While Atlanta in 1996 was arguably not the first Southern city to host an Olympics – St Louis in 1904 better deserves that distinction – the Atlanta games marked an important milestone in a tradition of challenges to racial barriers in the regional cities that have hosted Olympian spectacles. Nearly a century after St Louis, race and region remained firmly intertwined in American presentations of the Olympic games.

Disclosure statement

No potential conflict of interest was reported by the author.

ORCID

Mark Dyreson ⓘ http://orcid.org/0000-0002-4792-1072

Notes

1. For a variety of perspectives see George R. Matthews, *America's First Olympics: The St. Louis Games of 1904* (Columbia: University of Missouri Press, 2005); C. Robert Barnett, 'St. Louis 1904', in John Findling and Kimberly D. Pelle (eds), *Encyclopedia of the Modern Olympic Movement* (Westport, CT: Greenwood, 2004); Susan Brownell (ed.), *The 1904 Anthropology Days and Olympic Games: Sport, Race, and American Imperialism* (Lincoln: University of Nebraska Press, 2008); Bill Mallon, *The 1904 Olympic Games: Results for All the Competitors* (Jefferson, NC: Mcfarland, 1999); Robert K. Barney, 'Born From Dilemma: America Awakens to the Modern Olympic Games, 1901–1903', *Olympika* 1 (1992), 92–135; Linda S. Peavy and Ursula Smith, *Full-Court Quest: The Girls from Fort Shaw Indian School, Basketball Champions of the World* (Norman: University of Oklahoma Press, 2008); Mark Dyreson, 'The Playing Fields of Progress: American Athletic Nationalism and the St. Louis Olympics of 1904', *Gateway Heritage* 14, no. 2 (1993), 4–23; and Mark Dyreson, *Making the American Team: Sport, Culture, and the Olympic Experience* (Urbana: University of Illinois Press, 1998), 73–126.
2. Susan Brownell, *Bodies Before Boas: The 1904 St. Louis Olympic Games and Anthropology Days* (Lincoln: University of Nebraska Press, 2008); Lew Carlson, 'Giant Patagonians and Hairy Ainu: Anthropology Days at the 1904 St. Louis Olympics', *Journal of American Culture* 12 (Fall 1989), 19–26; Matti Gøksyr, '"One Certainly Expected a Great Deal More from the Savages": The Anthropology Days in St. Louis, 1904, and their Aftermath', *The International Journal of the History of Sport* 7, no. 2 (September 1990), 297–306; John Bale and Chris Philo (eds), *Body Cultures: Essays on Sport, Space, and Identity by Henning Eichberg* (London: Routledge, 1998); and Nancy J. Parezo and Don D. Fowler, *Anthropology Goes to the Fair: The 1904 Louisiana Purchase Exposition* (Lincoln: University of Nebraska Press, 2007).
3. Mark Dyreson, 'The "Physical Value" of Races: Anthropology and Athletics at the Louisiana Purchase Exposition', in Susan Brownell, *Bodies Before Boas: The 1904 St. Louis Olympic Games and Anthropology Days* (Lincoln: University of Nebraska Press, 2008), 114–40; Mark Dyreson, 'American Ideas about Race and Olympic Races from the 1890s to the 1950s: Shattering Myths or Reinforcing Scientific Racism?', *Journal of Sport History* 28, no. 2 (2001), 173–215.
4. Mark Dyreson, 'Showcases for Global Aspirations: Meditations on the Histories of Olympic Games and World's Fairs', *The International Journal of the History of Sport* 27, nos 16–18 (2010), 3037–44.
5. David Lunt and Mark Dyreson, 'The 1904 Olympic Games: Triumph or Nadir?', in Stephen Wagg and Helen Lenskyj (eds), *The Palgrave Handbook of Olympic Studies* (London: Palgrave, 2012), 44–59. The clearest expression of the thesis that St. Louis nearly ruined the Olympic movement can be found in the work of Karl Lennartz and Thomas Zawadzki. They indicted not only St. Louis but Paris in 1900 for nearly running the Olympic project into extinction. Karl Lennartz and Thomas Zawadzki, *Die Olympischen spiele 1906 in Athen* (Kassel: Kasseler Sportverlag, 1992); Karl Lennartz and Thomas Zawadzki, *Die Spiele der III. Olympiade 1904 in St. Louis* (Kassel: Agon-Sportverlag, 2004).
6. Webpage for Francis Stadium at Washington University site; http://bearsports.wustl. edu/facilities/francis-field (accessed 5 May 2015). A modest gymnasium built at the same time and used for some of the indoor sports at the 1904 Olympics, stands next door. Both were named after David R. Francis the former Missouri governor and US Secretary of Interior, who ran the World's Fair that housed the Olympics.

7. Bernd Hettlage, Wolfgang Reiher, and Sally Bixby Defty, *Olympic Stadium Berlin* (Berlin: Stadtwandel-Verl, 2006); David Hassan and Shakya Mitra (eds), *Olympic Games: Meeting New Global Challenges* (London: Routledge, 2015); Susan Brownell, *Beijing's Games: What the Olympics Mean to China* (Lanham, MD: Rowman & Littlefield, 2008); Guoqui Xu, *Olympic Dreams: China and Sports, 1895–2008* (Cambridge, MA: Harvard University Press, 2008); Chris Epting, *Los Angeles Memorial Coliseum* (Chicago, IL: Arcadia, 2002).

8. Aristea Papanicolaou-Christensen, *The Panathenaic Stadium: Its History over the Centuries* (Athens: Hellenic Republic – Ministry of Culture, General Secretariat for the Olympic Games: Historical and Ethnological Society of Greece, 2003); Alexander Kitroeff, *Wrestling With the Ancients: Modern Greek Identity and the Olympics* (New York: Greekworks, 2004); and Konstantinos Georgiadis, *Olympic Revival: The Revival of the Olympic Games in Modern Times* (Athens: Ekdotike Athenon, 2003).

9. Letter from W.J. Montgomery, Southern Pacific Lines, Detroit, Michigan, Traffic Department, to John H. Peatling, Sanitary Wax Paper Company, Kalamazoo, Michigan, 23 April 1932; Southern Pacific Brochures on California and the Olympic Games, MSS A90, File 1706, DeGolyer Library Special Collections, Southern Methodist University, Dallas, Texas.

10. As cited in John M. McGuire, 'Our Homegrown Olympiad', *St. Louis Post-Dispatch Sunday Magazine*, 3 July 1994, 8.

11. Steven Spearie, 'Forgotten Glory', *State Journal-Register* (Springfield, IL), 1 August 2004, 57.

12. McGuire, 'Our Homegrown Olympiad'; Spearie, 'Forgotten Glory'.

13. On Owens and his impact on national memory see William J. Baker, Jesse *Owens: An American Life* (New York: Free Press, 1986); David K. Wiggins, *Glory Bound: Black Athletes in a White America* (Syracuse, NY: Syracuse University Press, 2007); Mark Dyreson, 'Jesse Owens: Leading Man in Modern American Tales of Racial Progress and Limits', in David K. Wiggins (ed.), *Out of the Shadows: A Biographical History of the African American Athlete* (Fayetteville: University of Arkansas Press, 2006), 111–32; John Gleaves and Mark Dyreson, 'The "Black Auxiliaries" in American Memories: Sport, Race, and Politics in the Construction of Modern Legacies', *The International Journal of the History of Sport* 27, nos 16–18 (2010), 2893–924. On the Mexico City demonstrations and national and international memories see Douglas Hartmann, *Race, Culture, and the Revolt of the Black Athlete: The 1968 Olympic Protests and their Aftermath* (Chicago: University of Chicago Press, 2003); Amy Bass, *Not the Triumph But the Struggle: The 1968 Olympics and the Making of the Black Athlete* (Minneapolis: University of Minnesota Press, 2002); Kevin B. Witherspoon, *Before the Eyes of the World: Mexico and the 1968 Olympics* (DeKalb: Northern Illinois University Press, 2008).

14. John R. Gold and Margaret M. Gold (eds), *Olympic Cities: City Agendas, Planning and the World's Games, 1896–2016* (London: Routledge, 2011); John R. Gold and Margaret M. Gold (eds), *The Making of Modern Olympic Cities: Critical Concepts in Urban Studies* (London: Routledge, 2012); and Helen Lenskyj, *Inside the Olympic Industry: Power, Politics, and Activism* (Albany: State University of New York Press, 2000).

15. The Olympic Winter Games, from the origins, have often found homes in winter resorts looking to increase their global profile, from Chamonix and St. Moritz in the 1920s to Lake Placid, Squaw Valley, Grenoble, Innsbruck, Lillehammer, Nagano, Calgary, Salt Lake City, and Sochi, and many others in later decades. Gold and Gold (eds), *Olympic Cities*.

16. Kay Schiller and Chris Young, *The 1972 Munich Olympics and the Making of Modern Germany* (Berkeley: University of California Press, 2010); Ernie Troy, *Munich, Montreal and Moscow: A Political Tale of Three Olympic Cities* (Hove: Crabtree Press, 1980).

17. Washington, DC, and New York City have been pondering bids since the early 1900s, proposing a wide variety of potential stadium projects. Mark Dyreson, 'If We Build It Will They Will Come?: Washington National Stadium Schemes and American Olympic Desires', *The International Journal of the History of Sport* 25, no. 11 (2008), 1448–65. Philadelphia has pondered bids on numerous occasions, including in recent memory. Larry Eichel, 'No Regrets Over Failed Olympic Bid', *Philadelphia Inquirer*, 28 July 2006, B1; Marcia Gelbart, 'Philadelphia has Olympic Potential but Needs Work, Study Says', *Philadelphia Inquirer*, 14 July 2001, C1; Bob Ford, 'Olympic Dreams No Match for Reality', *Philadelphia Inquirer*, 10 May 2006, E1; Frank Fitzpatrick, 'Philly a Very Long Shot for

Olympics', *Philadelphia Inquirer*, 19 January 2014, E2; and Ramona Smith, 'Wharton Prof.: Hosting Olympics could Fight Blight', *Philadelphia Daily News*, 13 July 2001, A8.

18. US Census Bureau data on American cities in 1900, https://www.census.gov/population/www/documentation/twps0027/tab13.txt (accessed 10 March 2015).

19. The University of Chicago scholar John MacAloon remains displeased that St. Louis wrangled the Olympics away from Chicago. See his 'The 1904 Chicago-St. Louis Transition and the Social Structuration of the American Olympic Movement', in Russell Field (ed.), *Playing for Change: The Continuing Struggle for Sport and Recreation: Essays in Honour of Bruce Kidd* (Toronto: University of Toronto Press, 2015).

20. Mark Dyreson, 'The Endless Olympic Bid: Los Angeles and the Advertisement of the American West', *Journal of the West* 47, no. 4 (2008), 26–39; Mark Dyreson and Matthew Llewellyn, 'Los Angeles Is the Olympic City: Legacies of 1932 and 1984', *The International Journal of the History of Sport* 25, no. 14 (2008), 1991–2018. By the US census rankings of 1900, Los Angeles ranked 36th amongst the nation's cities, with a bit more than 100,000 inhabitants. By 1910, it had grown to 17th, at more than 300,000. In 1920, it ranked tenth, with more than half a million people. By 1930, Los Angeles had shot up to fifth, with 1.2 million residents. It remained fifth in the census of 1940, with 1.5 million inhabitants. It moved into fourth in 1950 with 1.9 million. By 1960, it was third, with nearly 2.5 million residents. US Census Bureau at http://www.census.gov/population/documentation/twps0027/tab13txt; http://www.census.gov/population/documentation/twps0027/tab14txt; http://www.census.gov/population/documentation/twps0027/tab15txt; http://www.census.gov/population/documentation/twps0027/tab16txt; http://www.census.gov/population/documentation/twps0027/tab17txt; http://www.census.gov/population/documentation/twps0027/tab18txt; http://www.census.gov/population/documentation/twps0027/tab19txt (accessed 25 January 2015).

21. Dyreson, 'The Endless Olympic Bid'; Dyreson and Llewellyn, 'Los Angeles Is the Olympic City'. US Census Bureau at http://www.census.gov/population/documentation/twps0027/tab21.txt; http://www.census.gov/population/documentation/twps0027/tab22.txt (accessed 10 February 2002).

22. David Rieff, *Los Angeles: Capital of the Third World* (New York: Simon & Schuster, 1991).

23. *Demographia* site on metropolitan statistical areas in the US, 1990–2000, http://www.demographia.com/db-usmet2000.htm (accessed 10 February 2015).

24. On modern Atlanta see Tomiko Brown-Nagin, *Courage to Dissent: Atlanta and the Long History of the Civil Rights Movement* (New York: Oxford University Press, 2011); Frederick Allen, *Atlanta Rising: The Invention of an International City, 1946–1996* (Atlanta: Longstreet Press, 1996); Kevin Michael Kruse, *White Flight: Atlanta and the Making of Modern Conservatism* (Princeton, NJ: Princeton University Press, 2005); and David L. Sjoquist (ed.), *The Atlanta Paradox* (New York: Russell Sage Foundation, 2000).

25. My argument is derived from some of the works that have 'rediscovered' the power of regionalism in American history, an eclectic group of scholars including Colin Woodard, *American Nations: A History of the Eleven Rival Regional Cultures of North America* (New York: Viking, 2011); Joel Garreau, *The Nine Nations of North America* (Boston: Houghton Mifflin, 1981); and David Hackett Fischer, *Albion's Seed: Four British Folkways in America* (New York: Oxford University Press, 1989). On the rise of the Sunbelt see Michelle Nickerson and Darren Dochuk (eds), *Sunbelt Rising: The Politics of Space, Place, and Region* (Philadelphia: University of Pennsylvania Press, 2011); Jon Smith and Deborah N. Cohn (eds), *Look Away!: The U.S. South in New World Studies* (Durham: Duke University Press, 2004); Sean P. Cunningham, *American Politics in the Postwar Sunbelt: Conservative Growth in a Battleground Region* (New York: Cambridge University Press, 2014); and Jon C. Teaford, *The Metropolitan Revolution: The Rise of Post-Urban America* (New York: Columbia University Press, 2006).

26. Tony Manfred, 'The Remote City That's Hosting the US-Portugal Game is the Most Glaring Example of World Cup Waste', http://www.businessinsider.com/manaus-world-cup-waste-2014-6#ixzz3VW51prHt (accessed 12 February 2015); Hadley Freeman, 'How Brazil's World Cup has Sold its People Short in the Amazon', *Manchester Guardian*, 17 June 2015.

27. Both the AOC and the AAU were headquartered before the Second World War in New York City. The 'Eastern Establishment' was heavily over-represented in the overlapping leadership of both groups as were American financiers headquartered in New York,

Philadelphia, Boston, and Chicago. For a comprehensive treatment see Robert E. Lehr, 'The American Olympic Committee, 1896–1940: From Chaos to Order' (PhD diss., Pennsylvania State University, 1985), 93–108. For biographies of the AOC and AOA leadership see John A. Lucas, 'Gustavus Town Kirby: Doyen of American Amateur Athletics and His Inadmissibility into the International Olympic Committee', *Stadion* 21–22 (1995–1996), 171–92; John A. Lucas, 'Architects of the Modernized American Olympic Committee, 1921–1928: Gustavus Town Kirby, Robert Means Thompson, and General Douglas MacArthur', *Journal of Sport History* 22 (Spring 1995), 38–45; John A. Lucas, 'Setting the Foundation and Governance of the American Olympic Association: The Efforts of Robert Means Thompson, 1911–1919 and 1922–1926', *Journal of Sport History* 29 (Fall 2002), 457–68. See also, Mark Dyreson, *Crafting Patriotism for Global Domination: America at the Olympic Games* (London: Routledge, 2009); Mark Dyreson, 'Selling American Civilization: The Olympic Games of 1920 and American Culture', *Olympika: The International Journal of Olympic Studies* 8 (1999), 1–41; and Mark Dyreson, 'Scripting the American Olympic Story-Telling Formula: The 1924 Paris Olympic Games and the American Media', *Olympika: The International Journal of Olympic Studies* 5 (1996), 45–80.

28.   Brown-Nagin, *Courage to Dissent*; Allen, *Atlanta Rising*; and Kruse, *White Flight*.

29.   'Gearing Up for Olympics – And for Scarlet Sequel Sticky Southern Heat Can't Dampen Expectations – A Letter from Atlanta', *Christian Science Monitor*, 6 August 1991.

30.   'Days of Glory and Heartbreak; World Attention Turns to Atlanta as the Summer Olympics Open', *Los Angeles Times*, 19 July 1996, B8.

31.   Patricia Cleary, *The World, the Flesh, and the Devil: A History of Colonial. St. Louis* (Columbia: University of Missouri Press, 2011); Adam Arenson, *The Great Heart of the Republic: St. Louis and the Cultural Civil War* (Cambridge, MA: Harvard University Press, 2011); Lincoln Steffens, *The Shame of the Cities* (New York: McClure, Phillips, 1904); and Eric Sandweiss, *St. Louis: The Evolution of an American Urban Landscape* (Philadelphia, PA: Temple University Press, 2001).

32.   Arenson, *The Great Heart of the Republic*. See also, Cyprian Clamorgan and Julie Winch, *The Colored Aristocracy of St. Louis* (Columbia: University of Missouri Press, 1999); Bryan M. Jack, *The St. Louis African American Community and the Exodusters* (Columbia: University of Missouri Press, 2007); Eric Sandweiss, *St. Louis in the Century of Henry Shaw: A View Beyond the Garden Wall* (Columbia: University of Missouri Press, 2003); and Frank Towers, *The Urban South and the Coming of the Civil War* (Charlottesville: University of Virginia Press, 2004).

33.   David R. Francis, *The Universal Exposition of 1904* (St. Louis: Louisiana Purchase Exposition Company, 1913), 312–13.

34.   Fair organizers scheduled 'Daughters of the Confederacy' Day for 7 October, a few days after the 'Union Veterans' Union' met at the fair on 4 October. *Official Guide to the Louisiana Purchase Exposition*, M.J. Lowenstein, compiler (St. Louis: Louisiana Purchase Exposition, 1904), 156. David R. Francis, president of the fair, tried to tone down obvious segregation but largely failed. He was proud there was no 'negro exhibit' to reinforce stereotypes but the black community recalls much segregation and racial affront, including cancellation of 'Negro Day'. The Pike had an 'Old Plantation' exhibit with caricatured versions of the carefree days of slavery. James Gilbert, *Whose Fair?: Experience, Memory, and the History of the Great St. Louis Exposition* (Chicago: University of Chicago Press, 2007), 83, 159.

35.   Matthews, *America's First Olympics*, 146.

36.   For a deeper development of this argument see Dyreson, *Making the American Team*; and Dyreson, *Crafting Patriotism*.

37.   Curiously a solid history of the Amateur Athletic Union remains to be written. Several interesting theses and dissertations have been produced, including Robert Korsgaard, 'A History of the Amateur Athletic Union of the United States' (PhD diss., University of Oregon, 1952); Lehr, 'The American Olympic Committee, 1896–1940'; and Daniel B. Reid, 'The Amateur Athletic Union of the United States and the Canadian Amateur Athletic Union, 1897–1914: A Study of International Sporting Relations' (MA diss., University of Western Ontario, 1990). One unpublished manuscript by the eminent historian of American amateur sport, John A. Lucas, also exists: John A. Lucas, 'The Amateur Athletic Union of the United States 1888–1988: A Century of Power and Progress', unpublished paper, 1989, copy in possession of the author.

38   *Official Handbook of the Amateur Athletic Union of the United States: Constitution, Bylaws, & General and Athletic Rules* (New York: American Sports Publishing, 1896), 22–3; Dale Somers, *The Rise of Sport in New Orleans, 1850–1900* (Baton Rouge: Louisiana State University Press, 1972), 244–5.

39.   For a particularly powerful analysis of this sacrifice in regards to sporting institutions in the United States see Charles Martin's masterful *Benching Jim Crow: The Rise and Fall of the Color Line in Southern College Sports, 1890–1980* (Urbana: University of Illinois Press, 2010). See also, David K. Wiggins, *Glory Bound: Black Athletes in White America* (Syracuse, NY: Syracuse University Press, 1997); David K. Wiggins and Patrick J. Miller, *The Unlevel Playing Field: A Documentary History of the African American Experience in Sport* (Urbana: University of Illinois Press, 2003).

40.   In 1992 LeRoy T. Walker, a longtime track coach who headed the U track team at the 1976 Montreal Olympics and had a doctorate in biomechanics from New York University, won election as president of the USOC. He served in that capacity until the end of the Atlanta games in 1996. Charles Gaddy, *An Olympic Journey: The Saga of an American Hero – LeRoy T. Walker* (Glendale, CA: Griffin Pub. Group, 1998).

41.   'New York Athletes' Victory Protested, *New York Times*, 4 September 1904, 10; J.W. McConaughy, 'Great Work Done by Athletes in the Stadium Events', *St. Louis Post-Dispatch*, 11 September 1904, Scrapbook 1904 B, United States Olympic Committee Archives. J.W. McConaughy, 'Chicago Protests New York's Victory in Olympic Games', *St. Louis Post-Dispatch*, 4 September 1904, 10; R.F. Baldwin, 'Chicago A.C. Officials Say That DeWitt is a "Ringer"', *St. Louis Star*, 4 September 1904, section 3, 1; 'Storm of Protests Mark N.Y.A.C.'s Victory by 1 Point in Olympic Games', *St. Louis Globe-Democrat*, 4 September 1904, 15; 'Chicago Men Beat C.A.A.', *Chicago Tribune*, 5 September 1904, 8; 'Great Olympic Games End at World's Fair', *Louisville Herald*, 4 September 1904, Scrapbook 1904 B, United States Olympic Committee Archives; 'World's Championship Trophy for N.Y.A.C.', *New York Times*, 22 November 1904, 7.

42.   St. Louis hosted three more championships after 1904 (1917, 1954, and 1963) while Los Angeles staged nine (1921, 1952, 1956, 1964, 1974, 1976, 1978, 1979, and 1984).

43.   Black athletes competed in championship meets in segregated cities as early as 1890 when a Philadelphia distance runner ran at Washington DC. Gregory Bond, 'Jim Crow at Play: Race, Manliness, and the Color Line in American Sports, 1876–1916' (PhD diss., University of Wisconsin-Madison, 2008), 422–30. On the Norfolk meet see James Edward Sullivan, comp., *Spalding's Official Athletic Almanac for 1908* (New York: American Sports Publishing Co., 1908) – Taylor's picture appears on page 51, results from Jamestown run from 39–55; and 'The Month', *Colored American Magazine*, 1 October 1907, 250. The magazine took the information from a 15 September 1907, article in the *New York Sun*, entitled, 'Taylor, Irish A.A.C.' See also 'Jamestown Games Please Sullivan', *New York Times*, 11 September 1907, 14; 'No Color Line in A.A.U. Sports. New College Rule Not Directed against J.B. Taylor', *Indianapolis Freeman*, 14 December 1907, 6. On the Baltimore meet see James Edward Sullivan, comp., *Spalding's Official Athletic Almanac for 1915* (New York: American Sports Publishing Co., 1915), 93–5; 'Gotham Juniors Win A.A.U. Title', *Chicago Tribune*, 12 September 1914, 10; 'Three New Records in Junior Games', *New York Times*, 12 September 1914, 10; 'Juniors Make Three Records', *Baltimore Sun*, 12 September 1914, 8; Adolph Commagere Wins Hammer Throw at Meet', *New Orleans Times Picayune*, 13 September 1914, 11; 'Loomis Star of Big Games', *Baltimore Sun*, 13 September 1914, MS1 and 4; 'Irish Americans Win Senior Meet', *New Orleans Times Picayune*, 13 September 1914, sec. 211; 'Irish-Americans Win Honors at A.A.U. Meet', *San Francisco Chronicle*, 13 September 1914, 57; 'Irish-Americans Still Champions', *New York Times*, 13 September 1914, S2; 'Senior Honors to Irish Team', *Chicago Tribune*, 13 September 1914, B1.

44.   'That New Amateur Rule', *Baltimore Sun*, 25 November 1907, 10.

45.   'No Color Line in A.A.U. Sports. New College Rule Not Directed Against J.B. Taylor', *The Freeman* (Indianapolis, Indiana), 14 December 1907, 6.

46.   On the Baltimore meet see James Edward Sullivan, comp., *Spalding's Official Athletic Almanac for 1915* (New York: American Sports Publishing Co., 1915), 93–5; 'Gotham Juniors Win A.A.U. Title', *Chicago Tribune*, 12 September 1914, 10; 'Three New Records in Junior Games', *New York Times*, 12 September 1914, 10; 'Juniors Make Three Records',

Baltimore Sun, 12 September 1914, 8; Adolph Commagere, 'Wins Hammer Throw at Meet', *New Orleans Times Picayune*, 13 September 1914, 11; 'Loomis Star of Big Games', *Baltimore Sun*, 13 September 1914, sec. MS1 and 4; 'Irish Americans Win Senior Meet', *New Orleans Times Picayune*, 13 September 1914, sec. 2, 11; 'Irish-Americans Win Honors at A.A.U. Meet', *San Francisco Chronicle*, 13 September 1914, 57; 'Irish-Americans Still Champions', *New York Times*, 13 September 1914, S2; 'Senior Honors to Irish Team', *Chicago Tribune*, 13 September 1914, B1.

47. On the East St. Louis race riots see Charles L. Lumpkins, *American Pogrom: The East St. Louis Race Riot and Black Politics* (Athens: Ohio University Press, 2008); Harper Barners, *Never Been a Time: The 1917 Race Riot that Sparked the Civil Rights Movement* (New York: Macmillan, 2008). On the evolution of the Civil Rights Movement in St. Louis see Clarence Lang, *Grassroots at the Gateway: Class Politics and Black Freedom Struggle in St. Louis, 1936–75* (Ann Arbor: University of Michigan Press, 2009). On the 1917 St. Louis meet see 'Joie Ray Lowers A.A.U. Mile Mark', *New York Times*, 2 September 1917, 15; *Spalding's Official Athletic Almanac for 1918* (New York: American Sports Publishing Co., 1918), 108–11; 'Glimpses of the A.A.U. Championships', *New Orleans Times Picayune*, 16 September 1917, B11; 'Chicago Athletes Again to the Fore', *Baltimore American*, 2 September 1917, 12.

48. 'Fitzpatrick Balks', *New Orleans Times Picayune*, 13 August 1910, 10. See also, Jodella K. Dyreson and Mark Dyreson, 'Clearing the Color Bar: The Battles of New Orleans and the Alamo (Stadium)', unpublished paper presented at the 42nd Annual Conference of the North American Society for Sports History, Glenwood Springs, CO, 31 May 2014.

49. 'Elks Indoor Baseball Team Anxious to Take on Y.M.H.A. in Series', *New Orleans Times Picayune*, 2 September 1910, 7; 'Re-Election of Old Officers by S.A.A.A.U.', *New Orleans Times Picayune*, 20 September 1910, 10; 'Negro Runner Dead: John B. Taylor, Quarter Miler, Victim of Typhoid Pneumonia', *New York Times*, 3 December 1908, 10; and 'Taylor, Noted Negro Athlete of Penn University Dies', *Boston Journal*, 3 December 1908, 9.

50. 'In and Around New York: Square Deal', *Chicago Defender*, 17 April 1926, 8.

51. 'A.A.U. Meeting Scheduled Here Is Called Off', *New Orleans Times Picayune*, 22 April 1927, 1, 6; Wm. McG. Keefe, 'Viewing the News', *New Orleans Times Picayune*, 22 April 1927, 15.

52. 'No Bar Negroes', *Chicago Daily Tribune*, 22 April 1927, 19; 'Secretary Rubien Issues Statement', *New Orleans Times Picayune*, 22 April 1927, 6.

53. 'Several Cities Bid for A.A.U. Games: Decision Not to Hold Meet at New York City', *New York Times*, 23 April 1927, 11; 'Lincoln, Neb., Seeking A.A.U. Championships', *New York Times*, 28 April 1927, 20; 'A.A.U. Favors Lincoln', *New York Times*, 29 April 1927, 18; 'A.A.U. Title Games for Lincoln, Neb.: Telegraph Vote Favors Selection', *New York Times*, 17 May 1927, 37; 'National A.A.U. Meet is Awarded to Lincoln, Neb.', *New Orleans Time Picayune*, 17 May 1927, 13.

54. On the new racially inclusive Southwestern AAU branch see George White, 'Sport Broadcast', *Dallas Morning News*, 13 March 1936, sec. 2, 7; 'Form Southwestern Division of A.A.U. at Local Meeting', *Dallas Morning News*, 9 May 1936, sec. 2, 3; George White, 'Sport Broadcast', *Dallas Morning News*, 10 May 1936, sec. 4, 5; 'Famed Negro Stars Compete'; 'A.A.U. Opens for Negroes', *Dallas Express*, 12 September 1936, 3. Tellingly, the articles in the *Dallas Morning News* do not mention that the new organization is open to all races, but the stories in the *Dallas Express* feature that fact prominently. On the meet itself see 'Metcalfe to Race in Juneteenth Meet', *Dallas Times Herald*, 16 June 1936, sec. 2, 7; Charles Burton, 'National Mark Is Smashed in Carnival Here', *Dallas Morning News*, 20 June 1936, sec. 2, 5; P.D. Whitted, 'Scrappy's Sport Scraps', *Dallas Express*, 27 June 1936, 3; 'White and Negro Trackmen to Compete in Carnival Tonight at Cotton Bowl', *Dallas Morning News*, 19 June 1936, sec. 2, 7–8; 'Famed Negro Stars Compete Friday Night', *Dallas Express*, 20 June 1936, 3; Louis Cox, 'Amateur Alley', *Dallas Times Herald*, 19 June 1936, sec. 2, 4; 'White, Negro Athletes to Vie in Track Meet at Cotton Bowl Friday', *Dallas Morning News*, 18 June 1936, sec. 2, 3; Jesse O. Thomas, 'First Interracial Tract Meet', *Dallas Express*, 27 June 1936, 3; Louis Cox, 'Famed Track Stars Compete Here Tonight', *Dallas Times Herald*, 19 June 1936, sec. 2, 6. See also, Jodella K. Dyreson and Mark Dyreson, 'The Racial Dynamics of the Forgotten Texas Centennial Olympic Games, 1936', unpublished paper presented at the 111th Annual Meeting of the Texas State Historical Association Meeting, 10 March 2007, San Antonio, TX.

55. 'Two Visiting Athletes Are 'Y' House Guests', *Dallas Express*, 17 July 1937, 3; 'Big Fair Takes on Color with Games Nearing', *Dallas Morning News*, 14 July 1937, sec. 1, 1, 12; 'All Eyes Turn to Exposition As Games Start', *Dallas Morning News*, 15 July 1937, sec. 1, 1, 3; Charles Burton, 'Pan-American Games to Open in Cotton Bowl Tonight', *Dallas Morning News*, 15 July 1937, sec. 2, 4, 9; 'Athletic Games Draw Attention at Exposition', *Dallas Morning News*, 13 July 1937, sec. 1, 1, 10; Jack Patton, 'Setting a New Record' cartoon, 15 July 1937; Pan-American Exposition, Sports – 1937 Folder, Vertical Files, Special Collections, Dallas Public Library, Dallas, Texas; 'Olympics Open with Earnest Note of Amity', *Dallas Morning News*, 16 July 1937, sec. 1, 1, 16; 'Warm Welcome Extended Opening Olympics', *Dallas Morning News*, 16 July 1937, sec. 2, 1; 'Noted Visitors See Big Games', *Dallas Morning News*, 17 July 1937, sec. 1, 10; Charles Burton, 'Track Stars of Americas Vie in Cotton Bowl Tonight', *Dallas Morning News*, 17 July 1937, sec. 2, 4; Charles Burton, 'Woodruff Shatter's World Record in 800-Meter Run', *Dallas Morning News*, 18 July 1937, sec. 4, p. 2, 13; John Lardner, 'Negro's Spurt Find's Western Ace All Spent', *Dallas Morning News*, 18 July 1937, sec. 4, 2; Eugene D. Sawyer, 'Woodruff Sets New Record', *Dallas Express*, 24 July 1937, 3; 'Athletes, Officials Praise Pan-American Games', 19 July 1937; Pan-American Exposition, Sports – 1937 Folder, Vertical Files, Special Collections, Dallas Public Library, Dallas, Texas; 'Brazil Want Pan-American Games in 1938', *Dallas Morning News*, 18 July 1937, sec. 1, 1, 9; 'Brazil Wants Games for Rio de Janeiro in '38, Official Says', *Dallas Morning News*, 18 July 1937, sec. 4, 2; George McClelland, 'Pan American Games Star Athletes', *Southwest Business* 16 (July 1937), 10–1, 22; 'Headliners of the Exposition', *Southwest Business* 16 (August 1937), 26. See also, Mark Dyreson, 'The First Pan American Olympics? The "Good Neighbor Policy", Pan American Politics, and the 1937 Athletic Spectacles at the Greater Texas and Pan American Exposition', unpublished paper presented at the Latin American Studies Association Annual Conference, Toronto, Canada, 8 September 2010; Mark Dyreson, '"Everything's Bigger in Texas": Ballyhoo, Bravado, and Identity at the Texas "Olympics" of 1936 and 1937', unpublished paper presented at the 35th Annual Conference of the North American Society for Sport History. Texas Tech University, Lubbock, Texas, 26 May 2007; Mark Dyreson and Jodella K. Dyreson, 'The Racial Dynamics of the Pan-American Olympics, 1937', unpublished paper presented at the 111th Annual Meeting of the Texas State Historical Association Meeting, 10 March 2007, San Antonio, TX.

56. 'San Antonio Gets Nat'l AAU Track Meet', *San Antonio Express*, 9 December 1945, C1. See also 'San Antonio Goes after National Track', *San Antonio Light*, 13 November 1945, A9; 'San Antonio to Get National Meet', *San Antonio Light*, 8 December 1945, A4; 'Boston Will Stage A.A.U. Ring Event', *New York Times*, 9 December 1945, sec. 5 (sports), 1; 'Boston is Given AAU Boxing in Stormy Session', *Chicago Daily Tribune*, 9 December 1945, A1; 'Clearing the Color Bar', *Opportunity*, April 1946, 90; Stanley Woodward, 'World of Sports', *New York Herald Tribune*, 7 January 1946; 'Switch the Track Meet', *New York Herald Tribune*, 15 January 1946; 'No AAU Games in Texas', *New York Amsterdam News*, 9 February 1946, 10, http://search.proquest.com/docview/226035683 (accessed 19 March 2014); Dan Burley, 'Negroes Asked to Help Break Ban on Boxing', *New York Amsterdam News*, 2 March 1946, 1, http://search.proquest.com/docview/225976802 (accessed 19 April 2014); 'NYAC Official Douses Lights to Hit Negroes', *New York Amsterdam News*, 6 April 1946, 1, available at http://search.proquest.com/docview/ 225950116 (accessed 19 April 2013); Dan Burley, 'Confidentially Yours', *New York Amsterdam News*, 13 April 1946, 12, http://search.proquest.com/docview/225959017 (accessed 19 April 2014); Dan Burley, 'Confidentially Yours', *New York Amsterdam News*, 26 January 1946, 17, http://search.proquest.com/docview/226019275 (accessed 19 April 2014); 'Former 600 Yard Champ Backs Burley's AAU Stand', *New York Amsterdam News*, 23 February 1946, 1, http://search.proquest.com/docview/225963000 (accessed 19 April 2014). See also Joe Cummiskey, 'Stars Over Texas, Cont'd', *New York PM*, 16 January 1946, 14; Don De Leighbur, 'New York Scribe Urges Negro Athletes to Come to S.A. for A.A.U. Meet', *San Antonio Register*, 1 February 1946, 3; 'Agitation against City As AAU Site, Scored', *San Antonio Register*, 25 January 1946, 3; Harold Scherwitz, 'Sportlights', *San Antonio Light*, 17 March 1946, D1; 'Albritton Enters AAU Meet, Here', *San Antonio Register*, 12 April 1946, 3; 'Sees Negroes in Meet', *New York Times*, 21 March 1946, 22; 'Grand St. Boys Join Pioneer Club in Banning National A.A.U. Track', *New York Times*, 20

June 1946, 29; 'Herbert Planning to Make San Antonio Trip', *New York Times*, 21 June 1946, 27; 'Clearing the Color Bar'; 'Negro Stars May Spurn Nat'l AAU Meet', *Pittsburgh Courier*, 12 January 1946, 16; 'Pioneer Club Bolsters Squad', *Chicago Defender*, 12 January 1946, 7; 'PM Opposes Texas AAU Track Meet', *Pittsburgh Courier*, 19 January 1946, 15; Fay Young, 'Through the Years', *Chicago Defender*, 19 January 1946, 7; Charley Cherokee, 'National Grapevine', *Chicago Defender*, 26 January 1946, 13; 'Some Top AAU Stars Will "Sell Out" to Dixie Bias', *Pittsburgh Courier*, 26 January 1946, 15; Fay Young, 'Through the Years', *Chicago Defender*, 9 February 1946, 9; 'Negro Stars Risk Race Pride for "Dinky" AAU Medals', *Pittsburgh Courier*, 29 June 1946, 36; 'Tickets on Sale at S.A. Register for AAU Meets', *San Antonio Register*, 7 June 1946, 3; 'Fleet-Footed Stars of the Cinder World Romping to Victory in Natl. AAU Meet in Texas', *Pittsburgh Courier*, 13 July 1946, 27; Joseph M. Sheehan, '300 Stars in Texas for Annual Meet', *New York Times*, 28 June 1946, 25; Associated Press, 'Thinclad Greats Compete in National AAU Track, Field Meet', *Corsicana Daily News*, 29 June 1946, 7; Ed Fite, 'Bill Cummins Face N.J. Hurdle Star', *El Paso Herald Post*, 29 June 1946, 6; Texans Take Major Share of AAU Honors', *Lubbock Morning Avalanche*, 29 June 1946, 7; Associated Press, 'Nation's Mightiest Track and Field Men Eye Records Today', *Harlingen Valley Morning Star*, 29 June 1946, 3; 'Discus Mark Shattered in National AAU', *Corpus Christi Caller-Times*, 30 June 1946, D1-2; 'Martineson High Scorer at AAU', *Laredo Times*, 30 June 1946, 8; Associated Press, 'Minnesota's Bob Fitch Establishes Record in Discus at San Antonio', *Big Spring Herald*, 30 June 1946, 8; Associated Press, 'Fitch, Strand Star at Track, Field Meet at Santone', *Galveston News*, 9. Velmo Ballenger, millionaire promoter of the meet and publisher of the *San Antonio Register*, provided for dining and sleeping accommodations for African-American competitors, officials, journalists, and coaches in private homes and saw to entertainment for them in nightspots such as the newly opened Suburban Club. Some national sportswriters crowed that indeed the black athletes were better off than their white competitors who were left 'on their own'. See Dan Burley, 'Confidentially Yours', *New York Amsterdam News*, 6 July 1946, 10, http://search.proquest.com/docview/226005060 (accessed 19 April 2014); 'Jo's Jottings', *San Antonio Register*, 3 May 1946, supp. 1, The Portal to Texas History, University of North Texas Libraries, Denton, Texas, from holdings from the University of Texas at San Antonio, San Antonio, TX, http://texashistory.unt.edu/ark:/67531/metapth399158/ (accessed 19 April 2014); U. Jay, 'Side Lights, High Lights of National AAU Meet', *San Antonio Register*, 5 July 1946, 3–4. See also, 'Dillard is Double Winner in National AAU Meet', *Chicago Defender*, 6 July 1946, 10; Johnny Janes, 'Minnesotan Sets World Discus Mark', *San Antonio Light*, 30 June 1946, B1, 3; U. Jay, 'Negroes Win 7 Senior, 4 Junior National AAU Titles: Harrison Dillard is Meet's Only Double Winner, Copping Both Hurdles', *San Antonio Register*, 5 July 1946, 3; Johnny Janes, 'Strand Heads Fancy Field in Senior Track', *San Antonio Light*, 29 June 1946, 4; Johnny Janes, 'Track Stars Battle at 6:45', *San Antonio Light*, 28 June 1946, A8; Lucius Jones, 'Negro Stars Dominate AAU Meet in San Antonio', *Pittsburgh Courier*, 6 July 1946, 27; 'Dillard Is Double Winner in National AAU Meet', *Chicago Defender*, 6 July 1946, 10; Fay Young, 'Through the Years', *Chicago Defender*, 6 July 1946, 11; 'Tickets on Sale at S.A. Register for AAU Meets', *San Antonio Register*, 7 June 1946, 3; Sheehan, '300 Stars'; 'Juniors to Open National Track Tourney Today', *Chicago Daily Tribune*, 28 June 1946, 29; 'Track Stars Open National Two Day Meet', *Chicago Daily Tribune*, 29 June 1946, 17; Joseph M. Sheehan, 'Bill Mack Takes 1500 Meter Run', *New York Times*, 29 June 1946, 14; Joseph M. Sheehan, 'Strand Beats MacMitchell', *New York Times*, 30 June 1946, sec. sports 1, 3; '"Stockholm Express" Pulls in Alone', *San Antonio Light*, 30 June 1946, B1; and 'A.A.U. Backers "In the Clear",' *San Antonio Light*, July 1946, 7. See also, Jodella K. Dyreson and Mark Dyreson, 'Clearing the Color Bar: The Battles of New Orleans and the Alamo (Stadium)', unpublished paper presented at the 42nd Annual Conference of the North American Society for Sports History, Glenwood Springs, CO, 31 May 2014.

57. In 1950 at the College Park meet Morgan State University, a historically black college in Maryland, and New York's Pioneer Athletic Club, one of the leading integrated clubs in the nation, placed in the top five of the team standings. Joseph Sheehan, 'Attlesey Betters World Track Mark', *New York Times*, 25 June 1950, 131. The African-American half-miler, Mal Whitfield, winner of the 1948 and 1952 Olympic gold medals in his specialty, starred in the 1954 St. Louis meet. In the 1963 meet the African-American

sprinter Bob Hayes set a world's record in the 100 yard dash. 'A. A. U. Meet Mark Set by Whitfield', *New York Times*, 20 June 1954, sports section, 1; Will Bradbury, 'Hayes Lowers World Record for 100-Yard Dash to 0:09.1 in A.A.U. Track', *New York Times*, 22 June 1963, 17.

58. Robert Eugene Mendelson and Ariela Manor, *The St. Louis Olympiad, 1984: Desirable? Feasible?* (Edwardsville: Center for Urban and Environmental Research and Services, Southern Illinois University at Edwardsville, 1977).

59. Neil Amdur, 'New York Among 3 U.S. Cities Still in Running for '84 Olympics', *New York Times*, 3 August 1977, 21.

Index

www.ingramcontent.com/pod-product-compliance
Ingram Content Group UK Ltd.
Pitfield, Milton Keynes, MK11 3LW, UK
UKHW010021280225
455677UK00023B/731